ASCENT®
CENTER FOR TECHNICAL KNOWLEDGE

AutoCAD® 2017 (R1)
Update for AutoCAD® 2015 & 2016
Users

Student Guide
Mixed Units - 1st Edition

AUTODESK.
Authorized Publisher

ASCENT - Center for Technical Knowledge®
AutoCAD® 2017 (R1)
Update for AutoCAD® 2015 & 2016 Users
Mixed Units - 1st Edition

Prepared and produced by:

ASCENT Center for Technical Knowledge
630 Peter Jefferson Parkway, Suite 175
Charlottesville, VA 22911

866-527-2368
www.ASCENTed.com

Lead Contributor: Michelle Rasmussen

ASCENT - Center for Technical Knowledge is a division of Rand Worldwide, Inc., providing custom developed knowledge products and services for leading engineering software applications. ASCENT is focused on specializing in the creation of education programs that incorporate the best of classroom learning and technology-based training offerings.

We welcome any comments you may have regarding this student guide, or any of our products. To contact us please email: feedback@ASCENTed.com.

The following are registered trademarks or trademarks of Autodesk, Inc., and/or its subsidiaries and/or affiliates in the USA and other countries: 123D, 3ds Max, Alias, ATC, AutoCAD LT, AutoCAD, Autodesk, the Autodesk logo, Autodesk 123D, Autodesk Homestyler, Autodesk Inventor, Autodesk MapGuide, Autodesk Streamline, AutoLISP, AutoSketch, AutoSnap, AutoTrack, Backburner, Backdraft, Beast, BIM 360, Burn, Buzzsaw, CADmep, CAiCE, CAMduct, Civil 3D, Combustion, Communication Specification, Configurator 360, Constructware, Content Explorer, Creative Bridge, Dancing Baby (image), DesignCenter, DesignKids, DesignStudio, Discreet, DWF, DWG, DWG (design/logo), DWG Extreme, DWG TrueConvert, DWG TrueView, DWGX, DXF, Ecotect, Ember, ESTmep, FABmep, Face Robot, FBX, Fempro, Fire, Flame, Flare, Flint, ForceEffect, FormIt 360, Freewheel, Fusion 360, Glue, Green Building Studio, Heidi, Homestyler, HumanIK, i-drop, ImageModeler, Incinerator, Inferno, InfraWorks, Instructables, Instructables (stylized robot design/logo), Inventor, Inventor HSM, Inventor LT, Lustre, Maya, Maya LT, MIMI, Mockup 360, Moldflow Plastics Advisers, Moldflow Plastics Insight, Moldflow, Moondust, MotionBuilder, Movimento, MPA (design/logo), MPA, MPI (design/logo), MPX (design/logo), MPX, Mudbox, Navisworks, ObjectARX, ObjectDBX, Opticore, P9, Pier 9, Pixlr, Pixlr-o-matic, Productstream, Publisher 360, RasterDWG, RealDWG, ReCap, ReCap 360, Remote, Revit LT, Revit, RiverCAD, Robot, Scaleform, Showcase, Showcase 360, SketchBook, Smoke, Socialcam, Softimage, Spark & Design, Spark Logo, Sparks, SteeringWheels, Stitcher, Stone, StormNET, TinkerBox, Tinkercad, Tinkerplay, ToolClip, Topobase, Toxik, TrustedDWG, T-Splines, ViewCube, Visual LISP, Visual, VRED, Wire, Wiretap, WiretapCentral, XSI.

NASTRAN is a registered trademark of the National Aeronautics Space Administration.

All other brand names, product names, or trademarks belong to their respective holders.

General Disclaimer:

Notwithstanding any language to the contrary, nothing contained herein constitutes nor is intended to constitute an offer, inducement, promise, or contract of any kind. The data contained herein is for informational purposes only and is not represented to be error free. ASCENT, its agents and employees, expressly disclaim any liability for any damages, losses or other expenses arising in connection with the use of its materials or in connection with any failure of performance, error, omission even if ASCENT, or its representatives, are advised of the possibility of such damages, losses or other expenses. No consequential damages can be sought against ASCENT or Rand Worldwide, Inc. for the use of these materials by any third parties or for any direct or indirect result of that use.

The information contained herein is intended to be of general interest to you and is provided "as is", and it does not address the circumstances of any particular individual or entity. Nothing herein constitutes professional advice, nor does it constitute a comprehensive or complete statement of the issues discussed thereto. ASCENT does not warrant that the document or information will be error free or will meet any particular criteria of performance or quality. In particular (but without limitation) information may be rendered inaccurate by changes made to the subject of the materials (i.e. applicable software). Rand Worldwide, Inc. specifically disclaims any warranty, either expressed or implied, including the warranty of fitness for a particular purpose.

AS-ACD1701-UPD1MU-SG   //   IS-ACD1701-UPD1MU-SG

Contents

Preface

The *AutoCAD 2017 Update for AutoCAD 2015 & 2016 Users* student guide teaches the new and enhanced features introduced in the AutoCAD® 2016 and AutoCAD® 2017 (R1) software. The topics covered range from general improvements and command enhancements to 3D modeling and collaboration enhancements.

Among the many changes in this release are changes to the general interface components, including the addition of the Start Tab, enhancements to tabs and panels, and changes to Autodesk® A360 collaboration and Help.

There are several updates to commands, such as dimensions, and various 3D tools, such as Point Clouds, Rendering, and editing previews.

Topics Covered

- Interface enhancements

- Command preview enhancements

- Dimension enhancements

- Point Cloud enhancements

- Rendering enhancements

- Customization updates in the Cloud

- Design Feed palette

- Direct access to A360 (Cloud)

Note on Software Setup

This student guide assumes a standard installation of the software using the default preferences during installation. Lectures and practices use the standard software templates and default options for the Content Libraries.

Students and Educators can Access Free Autodesk Software and Resources

Autodesk challenges you to get started with free educational licenses for professional software and creativity apps used by millions of architects, engineers, designers, and hobbyists today. Bring Autodesk software into your classroom, studio, or workshop to learn, teach, and explore real-world design challenges the way professionals do.

Get started today - register at the Autodesk Education Community and download one of the many Autodesk software applications available.

Visit www.autodesk.com/joinedu/

Note: Free products are subject to the terms and conditions of the end-user license and services agreement that accompanies the software. The software is for personal use for education purposes and is not intended for classroom or lab use.

Lead Contributor: Michelle Rasmussen

Specializing in the civil engineering industry, Michelle authors training guides and provides instruction, support, and implementation on all Autodesk infrastructure solutions, in addition to general AutoCAD.

Michelle began her career in the Air Force working in the Civil Engineering unit as a surveyor, designer, and construction manager. She has also worked for municipalities and consulting engineering firms as an engineering/GIS technician. Michelle holds a Bachelor's of Science degree from the University of Utah along with a Master's of Business Administration from Kaplan University.

Michelle is an Autodesk Certified Instructor (ACI) as well as an Autodesk Certified Evaluator, teaching and evaluating other Autodesk Instructors for the ACI program. In addition, she holds the Autodesk Certified Professional certification for Civil 3D and is trained in Instructional Design.

As a skilled communicator, Michelle effectively leads classes, webcasts and consults with clients to achieve their business objectives.

Michelle Rasmussen has been a Lead Contributor for the *AutoCAD Update* student guides since 2012.

In this Guide

The following images highlight some of the features that can be found in this Student Guide.

Practice Files

The Practice Files page tells you how to download and install the practice files that are provided with this student guide.

FTP link for practice files

Chapters

Each chapter begins with a brief introduction and a list of the chapter's Learning Objectives.

Learning Objectives for the chapter

Instructional Content

Each chapter is split into a series of sections of instructional content on specific topics. These lectures include the descriptions, step-by-step procedures, figures, hints, and information you need to achieve the chapter's Learning Objectives.

Side notes

Side notes are hints or additional information for the current topic.

Practice Objectives

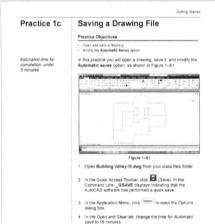

Practices

Practices enable you to use the software to perform a hands-on review of a topic.

Some practices require you to use prepared practice files, which can be downloaded from the link found on the Practice Files page.

Chapter Review Questions

Chapter review questions, located at the end of each chapter, enable you to review the key concepts and learning objectives of the chapter.

Command Summary

The Command Summary is located at the end of each chapter. It contains a list of the software commands that are used throughout the chapter, and provides information on where the command is found in the software.

Icons in this Student Guide

The following icons are used to help you quickly and easily find helpful information.

 | Indicates items that are new in the AutoCAD 2017 (R1) software.

 | Indicates items that have been enhanced in the AutoCAD 2017 (R1) software.

Practice Files

To download the practice files for this student guide, use the following steps:

1. Type the URL shown below into the address bar of your Internet browser. The URL must be typed **exactly as shown**. If you are using an ASCENT ebook, you can click on the link to download the file.

Address bar

ftp://ftp.ascented.com/cware/poecilia.zip

File   Edit   View   Favorites   Tools   Help

2. Press <Enter> to download the .ZIP file that contains the Practice Files.

3. Once the download is complete, unzip the file to a local folder. The unzipped file contains an .EXE file.

4. Double-click on the .EXE file and follow the instructions to automatically install the Practice Files on the C:\ drive of your computer.

   Do not change the location in which the Practice Files folder is installed. Doing so can cause errors when completing the practices in this student guide.

ftp://ftp.ascented.com/cware/poecilia.zip

Stay Informed!

Interested in receiving information about upcoming promotional offers, educational events, invitations to complimentary webcasts, and discounts? If so, please visit:

www.ASCENTed.com/updates/

Help us improve our product by completing the following survey:

www.ASCENTed.com/feedback

You can also contact us at: *feedback@ASCENTed.com*

User Interface

In this chapter you learn about changes made to the AutoCAD® software's user interface, specific commands, and software enhancements. Other changes include the addition of the *Start* Tab, and enhancements to the file and layout tabs, Status Bar, Ribbon, and Help.

Learning Objectives in this Chapter

- Locate changes to the basic layout and features of the AutoCAD software's user interface.
- Locate changes to specific commands in the AutoCAD software.
- Locate changes to the system configuration and performance of the AutoCAD software.

1.1 Interface Enhancements

Installation Enhancements

Autodesk Desktop Application

The Autodesk Application Manager has been replaced with the Autodesk Desktop Application (shown in Figure 1–1). Once the AutoCAD 2017 software installation is complete, the Autodesk Desktop Application opens automatically. It can also be accessed in the Windows desktop or in the Windows taskbar.

By logging into the Autodesk Desktop Application, you can access updates and learning content for products that you are subscribed to. Any updates or security patches that are available for all of the 2015, 2016, and 2017 Autodesk software installed on your computer are listed in this companion application.

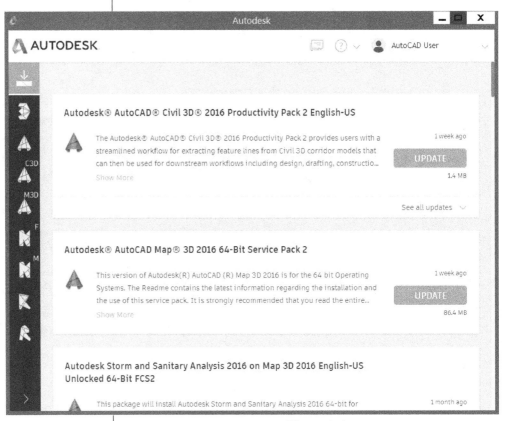

Figure 1–1

Migrate Custom Settings

A new tool is available which offers a more interactive way to migrate custom setting and files from earlier releases of the Autodesk software. The Migrate Custom Setting tool clearly identifies custom settings. This tool provides more control over which settings to migrate, as shown in Figure 1–2.

Figure 1–2

License Manager

The serial number and software key are now entered the first time the software is launched, rather than during installation. If anything changes after entering this information, the new License Manager enables you to easily change the license. The manager also lists the plug-ins, Add-ons, and extensions that are installed.

How To: Access the License Manager

1. In the Infocenter, expand the login option and select **Manage License**, as shown in Figure 1–3.

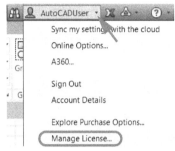

Figure 1–3

2. In the License Manager, expand the license information as shown in Figure 1–4.

Figure 1–4

3. Click **Change license type** to switch between a stand-alone license and a network license.

Dialog Box Enhancements

Several dialog boxes are bigger or can now be resized to display more information without having to scroll. To change the size of a dialog box, move the cursor to one of the corners until a double-arrow displays, as shown in Figure 1–5. Click and drag until the required size is set. You can also resize the dialog box by placing the cursor along one of the edges until a double-arrow displays, and then click and drag as required.

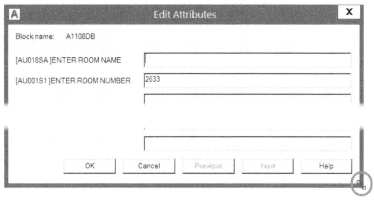

Figure 1–5

- Once set, the size of a dialog box is maintained each time the AutoCAD software is launched.

- Dialog boxes that are either larger or can be resized include the following:
  - Select File
  - Insert
  - Page Setup Manager
  - Object Grouping
  - Layer States Manager
  - Enhanced Attribute Editor
  - Edit Attributes
  - Move or Copy (Layout)
  - Drawing Properties
  - Security Options
  - Load/Unload Applications
  - Open VBA Project

Units

Survey units have been added as an option for the *Insertion scale* in the Drawing Units dialog box, as shown in Figure 1–6.

Figure 1–6

Tooltips

Tooltips display the item's name, a short description, and might include a graphic. They provide information about tools, commands, and drawing objects, as shown in Figure 1–7.

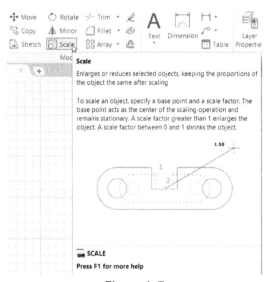

Figure 1–7

Tooltips can be toggled on or off and display delays can be set in the Options dialog box>*Display* tab>*Window Elements* area, as shown in Figure 1–8.

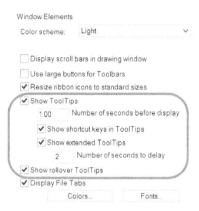

Figure 1–8

Start Tab

When you launch the AutoCAD software, the *Start* tab displays as shown in Figure 1–9.

Figure 1–9

The *Start* tab contains tools that enable you to start using the software by creating new drawings or opening existing, sample, or recently opened files. You can also connect to Autodesk® A360 to access online services.

- You can now access Recent Documents in both the *Start* tab and the Application Menu.

- The *Start* tab, which has replaced the Welcome Screen, opens when the software is launched.

- The *Start* tab displays on the left as you create and open additional drawings.

- You can press <Ctrl>+<Z> to return to the *Start* tab at any time.

- The **NEWTABMODE** system variable has been renamed to **STARTMODE**. When set to **0** (zero), the *Start* tab is no longer displayed.

- A new deployment option enables you to control if the *Start* tab is displayed or hidden for install deployments.

File Tabs

When multiple drawings are open, you have the ability to close them all at once rather than each one individually. When you right-click on a file tab, as shown in Figure 1–10, three options are displayed:

- **Close:** Closes only the active drawing file.

- **Close All:** Closes all drawing files and displays the *Start* tab.

- **Close All Other Drawings:** Closes all drawing files except for the currently active drawing file.

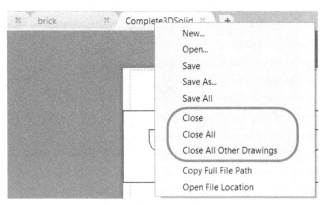

Figure 1–10

In addition to the three selections, two new commands are available for closing drawing files. You can now type **CLOSEALLOTHER** or **CLOSEALL** in the command line, as shown in Figure 1–11.

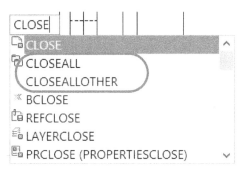

Figure 1–11

Layout Tabs

When repositioning layout tabs, you can now drag layouts into positions that are currently hidden by the overflow menu. As a layout is dragged to the edge of the displayed layout tabs (either on the left or right as shown in Figure 1–12), tabs automatically scroll to show hidden layouts. This enables you to drop a layout to any new location required.

Figure 1–12

Ribbon Galleries

Last year, various drop-down lists available in the Ribbon were replaced with galleries in which images of the available options are displayed. The new variable **GALLERYVIEW** can toggle Ribbon Galleries on or off.

- When the **GALLERYVIEW** variable is set to **0** (zero):
    - The preview is hidden, as shown on the left in Figure 1–13.
    - To display the Insert dialog box, click **Insert**.
- When the **GALLERYVIEW** variable is set to **1** (one):
    - The preview is toggled on, as shown on the right in Figure 1–13.
    - To display the Insert dialog box, at the bottom of the preview click **More Options...**.

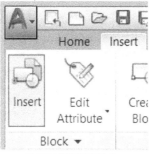

GALLERYVIEW=0

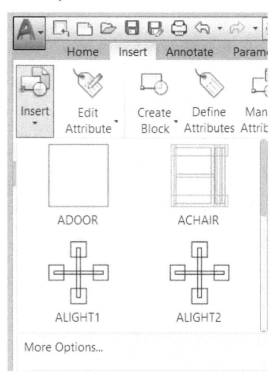

GALLERYVIEW=1

Figure 1–13

The Insert dialog box has been enlarged and reorganized, as shown in Figure 1–14. The updated dialog box displays a larger preview image and enables you to enter more characters in the *Name* field. The *Name* field now also supports Autocomplete, which reduces the need to scroll through the block list.

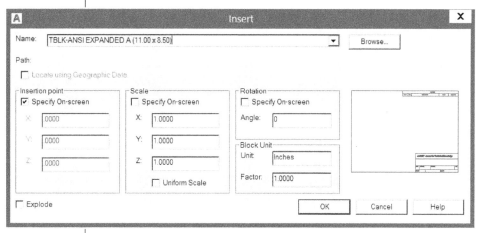

Figure 1–14

Status Bar

The Status Bar now wraps automatically to a second row if the software window shrinks or if addition buttons are displayed in the Status Bar. This ensures that all of the buttons are available across the bottom of the AutoCAD software window. Figure 1–15 shows the Status Bar wrapped to a second line. Additionally, the *Model* tab and at least one layout tab are always displayed.

Figure 1–15

Two additional command buttons have been added to the Status Bar: **Lock UI** and **Isolate Objects**. To display them, click **Customization** in the Status Bar and click each one, as shown in Figure 1–16.

Figure 1–16

Lock UI

The **Lock UI** button locks the position and the size of toolbars and dockable windows such as the DesignCenter or Properties palette. The **Lock UI** button now enables you to check/uncheck multiple UI elements at the same time rather than reopening the flyout each time. When you check an item, that specific type of user interface element becomes locked. Figure 1–17 shows all elements checked (locked).

Figure 1–17

Isolate Objects

The **Isolate Objects** button enables you to hide a specific object or hide all objects except for the selected one(s). The example in Figure 1–18 shows the options that are available before (on the left) and after (on the right) an object has been isolated or hidden.

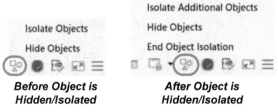

Figure 1–18

Help

Access to Help content and tools has been improved. Thanks to improved single sign-in capabilities, when signed into your A360 account, you are also automatically signed into Help documentation. Once singed into Help documentation, you can **Like** a topic to help you find it quicker in the future.

UI Finder

In the Help window, a Find link causes the Ribbon, Quick Access toolbar, Application Menu, and Status Bar to display an arrow showing where the command that you were searching for is located. Figure 1–19 shows a search of the **Insert** command and an arrow pointing to where it can be found.

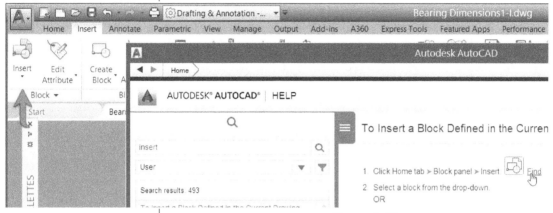

Figure 1–19

If the icon is located in the Status Bar but is not currently displayed, the UI finder points to the Customization icon In the Status Bar, as shown in Figure 1–20.

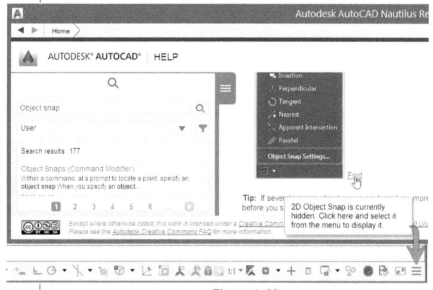

Figure 1–20

Practice 1a | User Interface Enhancements

Practice Objective

* Explore the AutoCAD software interface enhancements.

Estimated time for completion: 10 minutes

In this practice, you will explore the AutoCAD software user interface enhancements such as the *Start* tab, file tabs, layout tabs, Ribbon Galleries, Status Bar, and Help.

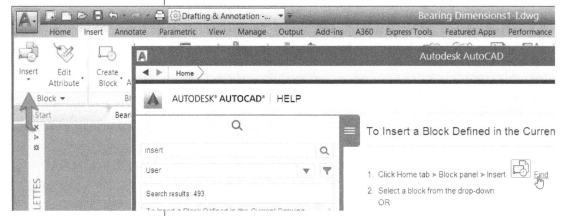

Figure 1–21

Task 1 - Work with tabs.

1. In the *Start* tab, open the *Create* tab, and then click **Open Files...**

2. In the Select Files dialog box, press <Ctrl> and select **Building Rock.dwg**, **Building Side.dwg**, **Building Valley.dwg**, and **HatchEdit-I.dwg** from the practice files folder. Click **Open**.

   The files display in tabs, as shown in Figure 1–22.

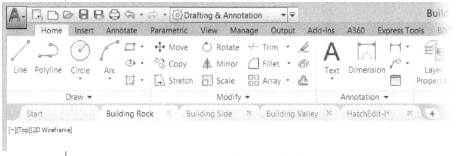

Figure 1–22

3. Select the *Building Rock* tab to make the **Building Rock.dwg** the active drawing.

4. Right-click on the *HatchEdit-I* tab and select **Close All Other Drawings**, as shown in Figure 1–23. The **HatchEdit-I.dwg** becomes the active drawing file and all other drawings are closed.

Figure 1–23

5. At the bottom of the AutoCAD window, select the *B-sized* layout tab. Hold <Ctrl> as you drag and drop the layout after Layout15, as shown in Figure 1–24.

Figure 1–24

Task 2 - Modify the User Interface.

1. Continue working in the **HatchEdit-I.dwg** or reopen it from the practice files if required.

2. Click on **Layout1** to make it active.

3. In the command line, type **GALLERYVIEW**. Change the value to **0** (zero).

4. In the InfoCenter, type **Insert** and press <Enter> to open the Help dialog box.

5. In the Help dialog box, select the **Insert** command topic on the left, then click the UI finder link on the right, as shown in Figure 1–25. An arrow is displayed in the Ribbon pointing to the **Insert** command.

Figure 1–25

6. Close the Help screen.

7. In the *Insert* tab>Block panel, click **Insert**. The Insert dialog box is displayed. Click **Cancel**.

8. In the command line, type **GALLERYVIEW**. Change the value to **1**.

9. In the *Insert* tab>Block panel, click **Insert**. In the Gallery, click **TBLK-ANSI EXPANDED A (11.00 X 8.50)**, as shown in Figure 1–26.

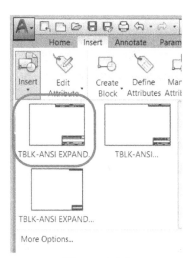

Figure 1–26

10. Type **0,0** in the command line for the insertion point and press <Enter>.

11. In the Status Bar, click ☰ (Customization). In the menu, select **Lock UI** and **Isolate Objects**, as shown in Figure 1–27, to display them in the Status Bar.

Figure 1–27

12. Change the size of the AutoCAD software window by making it smaller. Notice how the Status Bar wraps to a second line as the window gets too small to display all of the icons, as shown in Figure 1–28.

Figure 1–28

13. Close the drawing without saving.

1.2 Command Enhancements

Pickfirst

The PICKFIRST system variable controls whether you can select objects before starting a command. If the PICKFIRST system variable is set to 0 (zero), when you press <Delete> the message in Figure 1–29 displays. The Delete Key message can be toggled off by selecting **Always perform my current choice**. This adds it to the Hidden Message Settings.

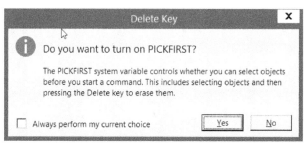

Figure 1–29

How To: Toggle the Delete Key Message On

1. In a blank space of the drawing window, right-click and select **Options**.
2. In the Options dialog box>*System* tab, click **Hidden Messages Settings**.
3. In the *Check message to show:* area, select **Delete Key** (as shown in Figure 1–30) and then click **OK**.

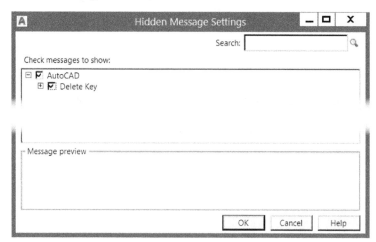

Figure 1–30

Hatch Layer

Using the HPLAYER system variable, you can set the layer on which the hatch is placed, overriding the current layer. If the layer you want to use does not exist in the drawing, type the new layer name, as shown in Figure 1–31. The next time the Hatch command is started, the layer is created and the hatch is placed on it.

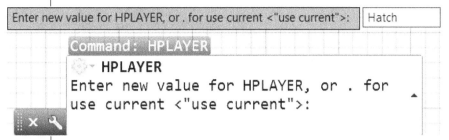

Figure 1–31

Command Preview

Command preview enables you to see the results of a command before committing to it. Previous releases provided this capability for Trim, Extend, Fillet, and Chamfer. The AutoCAD software provides a preview for the following commands:

- Blend

- Erase

- Rotate

- Scale

- Stretch

Blend

The **Blend** command combines two selected lines or curves by creating a spline in the gap between them.

How To: Blend Curves

1. In the *Home* tab>Modify panel>expand Fillet, select

    (Blend Curves).
2. The AutoCAD software prompts you to *Select first object:*.
   Position the cursor so that the small pick box is directly over
   the object to be blended near the endpoint, as shown in
   Figure 1–32. The object is highlighted in a thicker line weight.

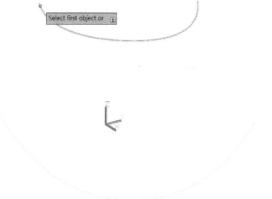

Figure 1–32

3. Select the object, which is then highlighted in blue.
4. The AutoCAD software prompts you to *Select second object:*.
   Position the cursor so that the small pick box is directly over
   the object to be blended near the endpoint, as shown in
   Figure 1–33. The object is highlighted in a thicker blue line
   weight, and the new spline is displayed.

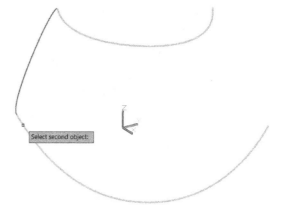

Figure 1–33

5. Select the object to end the command and combine the two
   objects.

Erase

The **Erase** command removes objects from the drawing file.

How To: Erase an Object

1. In the *Home* tab>Modify panel, click ✎ (Erase).
2. The AutoCAD software prompts you to *Select objects:*. Position the cursor so that the small pick box is directly over the object to be erased, as shown in Figure 1–34. The cursor displays ✕, indicating that the object is going to be erased, and the object is faded in a light gray line weight.

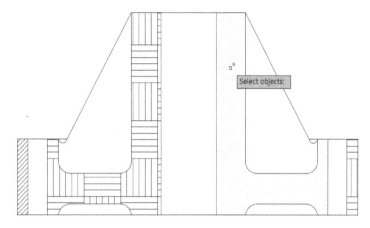

Figure 1–34

3. Continue selecting all of the objects to be erased.

    The erased objects remain in a light gray line weight until the command is completed.

4. Press <Enter> or right-click to erase the objects and complete the command.

Rotate

The **Rotate** command rotates selected objects around a defined pivot point.

How To: Rotate an Object

1. In the *Home* tab>Modify panel, click ⟳ (Rotate).
2. Select the objects to rotate.
3. Press <Enter> to end the object selection.

4. Select the base point around which the objects are going to rotate.

5. Move the cursor to rotate the objects. A dashed line indicates the location of the base point. ⏚ displays at the cursor, indicating that the **Rotate** command is active, as shown in Figure 1–35. It also indicates the direction in which typed values are going to be rotated, in this case, counter-clockwise. The original objects fade to gray while the new objects maintain their original properties.

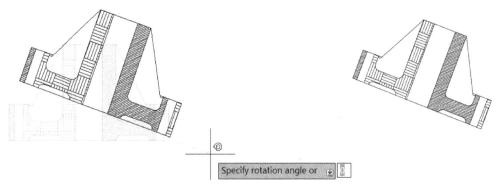

Type an angle value　　　　　　　　　　　　*Rotated object*

Figure 1–35

Scale

The **Scale** command enlarges or reduces the size of selected objects around a defined reference point.

How To: Scale an Object

1. In the *Home* tab>Modify panel, click ▭ (Scale)
2. Select the objects to scale.
3. Press <Enter> to end the object selection.
4. Select the base point to be used for scaling.
5. Move the cursor to scale the objects. ⬒ displays at the cursor, indicating that the **Scale** command is active, as shown in Figure 1–36. The original objects fade to gray while the new objects maintain their original properties.

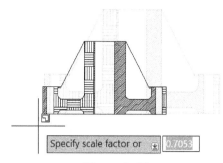

Figure 1–36

6. Type a value for the scale factor.

Stretch

The **Stretch** command enables objects and/or parts of objects to be moved and/or extended, leaving other objects and parts of objects stationary.

How To: Stretch Objects

1. In the *Home* tab>Modify panel, click ⌐ (Stretch).
2. Use a crossing selection to select the objects to stretch. The objects are displayed in blue.
3. Press <Enter> to finish the selection set.
4. Select the base point (the handle by which you hold the objects).
5. Move the cursor in the direction in which you want to stretch the object. A preview displays where the original objects fade to gray while the new objects maintain their original properties, as shown in Figure 1–37.

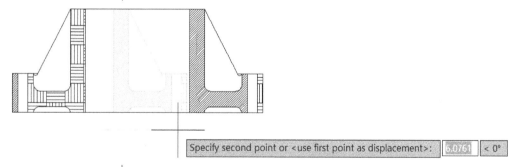

Figure 1–37

6. Select the second point (which in conjunction with the base point defines the distance and direction in which you are stretching) or type a distance value and press <Enter>.

Object Snaps

Object snaps enable you to take advantage of geometrical precision by snapping to exact points on objects, while you are in a command. The geometric center object snap tool now finds the geometric center (centroid) of a closed polyline. The osnap tooltip displays the label **Geometric Center** for the geometric center of the object, as shown in Figure 1–38.

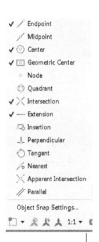

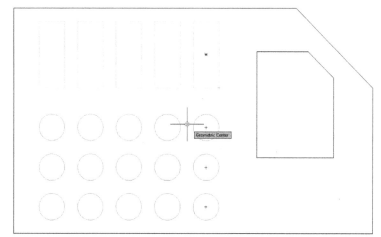

Figure 1–38

If the closed polyline contains arcs, hovering over an arc displays the tooltip label, **Center**, as shown on the left in Figure 1–39. Hovering over a circle displays the tooltip label, **Center**, as it always has (as shown on the right in Figure 1–39).

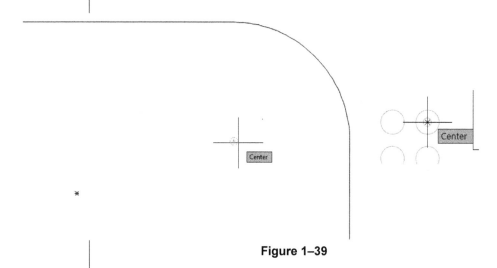

Figure 1–39

The object tracking glyph has also been updated to distinguish the geometric center object snap from other object snaps that display the traditional "+" glyph, as shown in Figure 1–40.

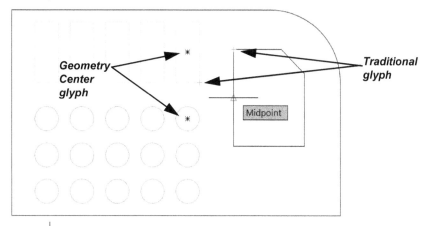

Figure 1–40

Xref Enhancements

In order to clearly distinguish which layers come from referenced drawings and which layer reside in the active drawing, xref layers are now shown in gray text in the *Home* tab>Layers panel>Layers drop-down list, as shown in Figure 1–41. Additionally, you can only change the visibility of xref layers in the layer panel drop-down list.

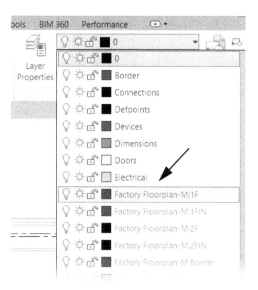

Figure 1–41

Xref layers have been removed from the Properties palette since they cannot be selected. Figure 1–42 shows the Properties palette for the same drawing shown in Figure 1–41. Notice that the **Factory Floorplan-M|** layers are all missing from the Layers drop-down list in the Properties palette.

Figure 1–42

You can now control the display of layers for objects in an xref drawing that were not set to "ByLayer" for the layer property updates in the original xref. The new **XREFOVERRIDE** variable enables objects in the reference file to override properties set in the drawing file it is referenced into (host file). Setting the **XREFOVERRIDE** to **1** enables the original file to set the properties. Setting the **XREFOVERRIDE** to **0** enables the drawing in which it is referenced to control the properties.

Practice 1b

Command Enhancements

Practice Objective

- Explore the AutoCAD software command enhancements.

Estimated time for completion: 20 minutes

In this practice, you will use some of the enhanced AutoCAD commands, such as **Blend Curves**, **Erase**, **Rotate**, **Scale**, **Stretch**, and polyline centroids.

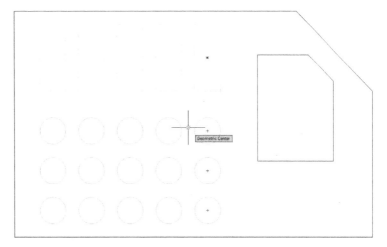

Figure 1–43

Task 1 - Use the Blend Curve command.

1. Open the **NURBS-M.dwg** from the practice files.

2. In the *Home* tab>Modify panel, expand the Fillet drop-down list and select ↗ (Blend Curve).

3. The AutoCAD software prompts you to *Select first object:*. Position the cursor so that the small pick box is directly over the top curve near the left endpoint, as shown in Figure 1–44. The object is highlighted in a thicker line weight.

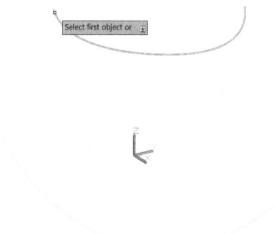

Figure 1–44

4. Select the object, which is then highlighted in blue.

5. The AutoCAD software prompts you to *Select second object:*. Position the cursor so that the small pick box is directly over the bottom curve near its left endpoint, as shown in Figure 1–45. The object is highlighted in a thicker blue line weight and the new spline is displayed.

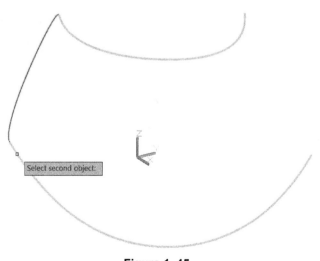

Figure 1–45

6. Select the object to end the command and combine the two objects.

Task 2 - Use the Erase command.

1. Continue working in the same drawing as the last step.

2. In the *Home* tab>Modify panel, click ✎ (Erase).

3. The AutoCAD software prompts you to *Select objects:*. Position the cursor so that the small pick box is directly over the spline you created in the last task, as shown in

    Figure 1–46. The cursor displays ✕, indicating that the object is going to be erased, and the object is faded in a light gray line weight.

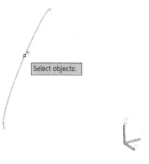

Figure 1–46

4. Select the object, press <Enter> or right-click to erase the spline and complete the command.

Task 3 - Use the Rotate command.

1. Open the **HatchEdit-I.dwg** from the practice files.

2. In the *Home* tab>Modify panel, click ↻ (Rotate).

3. Select all of the objects in the drawing and press <Enter> to end the object selection.

4. Select a point near the bottom right corner of the objects for the base point around which the objects are going to rotate.

5. Move the cursor to rotate the objects, as shown in Figure 1–47. The original objects fade to gray while the new objects maintain their original properties.

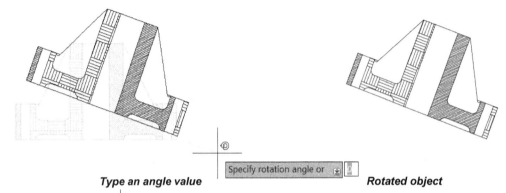

Type an angle value   Specify rotation angle or   *Rotated object*

Figure 1–47

6. Click to complete the rotation.

7. Press <Ctrl>+<Z> to undo the command.

Task 4 - Use the Scale command.

---

1. Continue working in the same drawing as the last task.

2. In the *Home* tab>Modify panel, click ⬚ (Scale).

3. Select all of the objects in the drawing and press <Enter> to end the object selection.

4. Select a base point near the bottom left corner to be used for scaling.

5. Move the cursor to scale the objects. ⬚ displays at the cursor, indicating that the **Scale** command is active, as shown in Figure 1–48. The original objects fade to gray while the new objects maintain their original properties.

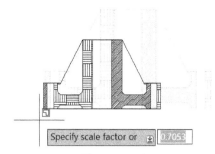

Figure 1–48

6. Type a value for the scale factor and press <Enter> to end the command.

Task 5 - Use the Stretch command.

1. Continue working in the same drawing as the last task.

2. In the *Home* tab>Modify panel, click ⌐ (Stretch).

3. Use a crossing selection to select the right half of the drawing to stretch. The objects turn blue.

4. Press <Enter> to finish the selection set.

5. Select any point as the base point (the handle by which you hold the objects).

6. Move the cursor to the right to stretch the object. A preview displays where the original objects fade to gray while the new objects maintain their original properties, as shown in Figure 1–49.

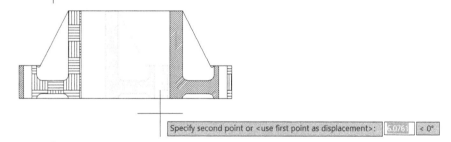

Figure 1–49

7. Type **6** and press <Enter> to end the command.

8. Close the drawing without saving.

Task 6 - Find the polyline centroid.

1. Open the **Select-M.dwg** from the practice files.

2. In the *Home* tab>Draw panel, click ✏ (Line).

3. Hold <Ctrl> as you right-click with the mouse.

4. Select **Geometric Center** from the list of Osnap overrides.

5. In the model, hover the cursor over the outer polyline, as shown in Figure 1–50. Click to accept the geographic center osnap.

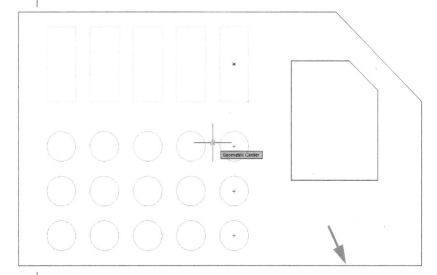

Figure 1–50

6. Press <Esc> to cancel the command.

1.3 Software Enhancements

Improved Graphics

The appearance of linetypes, lineweights, and curves has been improved. Linetypes with dots now display as round dots, rather than short dashes. When in the 2D Wireframe visual style, continuous lines and curves display perfectly at any zoom level, as shown in Figure 1–51. This means that you are no longer required to manually use the **Regen** command when zooming and panning. The **REGENAUTO** system variable automatically performs the regens as required.

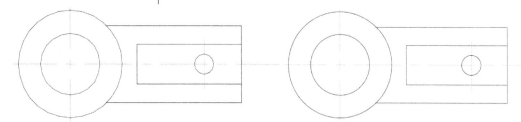

Figure 1–51

Hint: Graphics Hardware

Hardware acceleration must be toggled on and your graphics hardware must be DirectX11 capable.

2D Performance

The hidden system variable 2DRETAINMODE controls graphic caching.

2D graphics now take advantage of the Graphics Processing Unit (GPU) that is available in several of the newer display adapters. Graphics are cached in the GPU memory (rather than the CPU memory), which often makes pan and zoom operations faster and smoother.

Hint: Checking the Graphics Adapter

To use the 2DRETAINMODE, your graphics adapter must have at least 128 MB of GPU memory, otherwise the variable does not take effect.

To see how much GPU memory you have, open the computer's Control Panel. Then:

- **In Windows 7:** Click Appearance and Personalization> Display>Adjust screen resolution>Advanced settings.

- **In Windows 10:** Click Display>Adjust resolution>Advanced settings.

In the Adapter Information dialog box, you can view how much *Dedicated Video Memory* is available, as shown in Figure 1–52.

Figure 1–52

3D Performance

The stability of 3D navigation tools and the performance of 3D block have been improved by replacing the subsystem responsible for 3D interaction and adaptive degradation.

Command Preview

The overall performance for previewing changes to object properties has been improved. When a large number of objects are selected, the preview of any property changes are displayed much faster than in previous versions. This enables you to see the change before committing to it with much less lag time. When previewing a command, line smoothing displays the same as when the operation is completed.

How To: Modify Properties

1. Select the object(s) in the drawing file that you want to change.
2. In the *Home* tab>Properties panel, select the drop-down list for the property you want to change. Figure 1–53 shows the Color drop-down list expanded. Move the cursor over the options in the property drop-down list. The selected object(s) are displayed in the model as if they have been changed.

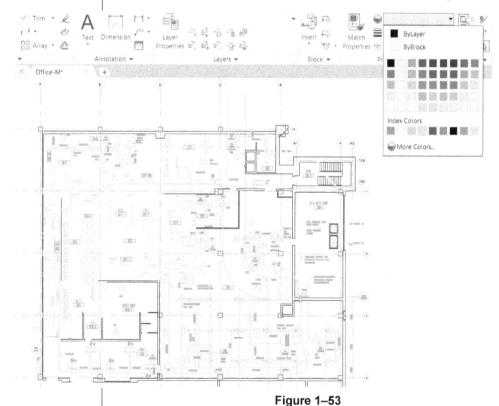

Figure 1–53

3. In the Property drop-down list, click on the new property to accept the preview and make the change.

Move/Copy

When selecting several objects to move or copy, a preview of the objects is created much faster than earlier releases, reducing lag time, as shown in Figure 1–54. This enables you to move the cursor freely with the objects attached to it, without waiting for the model to regen each time the cursor moves.

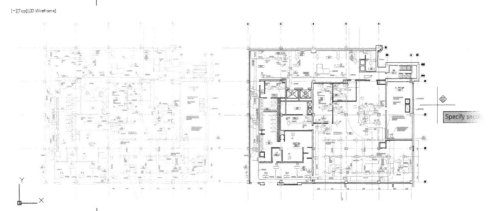

Figure 1–54

> **Hint: Visual Style**
>
> The visual style must be in 2D Wireframe in order to see a performance improvement.

Selection Highlighting

A new system variable controls the glowing selection highlighting effect color.

> **Hint: Hardware Acceleration**
>
> Hardware acceleration must be toggled on to use this feature.

How To: Change the selection effect color

1. Open the **Options** dialog box.
2. Click the *Selection* tab to make it active.

3. Expand the Selection effect color drop-down list, as shown in Figure 1–55, and select a new color.

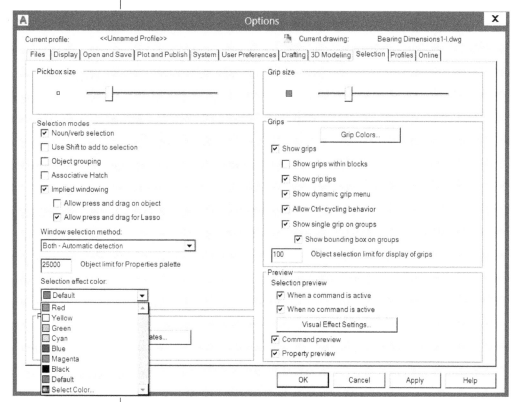

Figure 1–55

Cursor Badges

The new system variable, **CURSORBADGE**, enables you to toggle cursor badges on and off, as shown in Figure 1–56.

- Visible: To toggle cursor badges on, set the variable to **2**.

- Hidden: To toggle cursor badges off, set the variable to **1**.

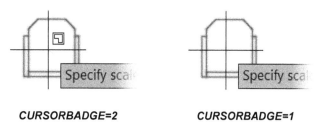

CURSORBADGE=2   *CURSORBADGE=1*

Figure 1–56

Improve Graphics Performance

You can now take advantage of the improved graphics for capable devices with a new control in the Graphics Performance dialog box.

How To: Improve Graphics Performance

1. Open the **Options** dialog box.
2. Click the *System* tab to make it active.
3. Click **Graphics Performance**.
4. In the Graphics Performance dialog box, check the option to use **High quality geometry (for capable devices)**, as shown in Figure 1–57.

Figure 1–57

- To access the Graphics Performance dialog box from the status bar, right-click on ⬤ (Hardware acceleration) and select **Graphics Performance...**, as shown in Figure 1–58.

Figure 1–58

System Variable Monitor

A new System Variable Monitor enables IT and CAD managers to quickly identify and edit variables that do not conform to a company's standards. When the **SYSVARMONITOR** command is active, a table is displayed indicating which system variables are selected to be monitored, as shown in Figure 1–59.

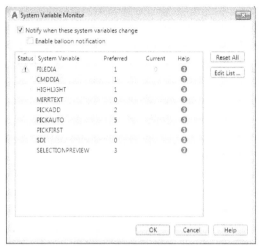

Figure 1–59

- The *Status* column displays ⚠ (Warning) next to monitored system variables that deviate from the preferred value.

- The *System Variable* column provides the names of the variables that are currently being monitored.

- The *Preferred* column indicates the preferred setting for the system variable.

- The *Current* column lists the current value for any system variables that are not equal to the preferred value.

- Selecting the option **Notify when these system variables change** evokes a notification in the command line when a monitored system variable violates a preferred setting, as shown in Figure 1–60.

Figure 1–60

- Selecting the option **Enable balloon notification** evokes a notification at the status bar when a monitored system variable violates a preferred setting, as shown in Figure 1–61.

Figure 1–61

How To: Monitor System Variables

1. Type **SYSVARMONITOR** to open the System Variable Monitor dialog box.
2. In the System Variable Monitor dialog box, click **Edit List**.
3. In the Edit System Variable List dialog box, select the variable you want to monitor from the available system variables list on the left, as shown in Figure 1–62. The list can be narrowed by typing in the *Search list* field at the top.

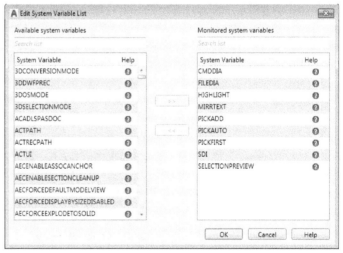

Figure 1–62

4. Click [>>] (Add Selected) to add the variable to the Monitored system variable list on the right.
5. Continue adding system variable to the list on the right and click **OK** when done.

Security Options

A new Security Options dialog box enables you to make adjustments to the security level using a control slider, as shown in Figure 1–63. To access this dialog box, in Options>*System* tab, click **Security Options**. In the Security Options dialog box, you can add and remove trusted folders for executable files. When searching for executable files, you can select from the following two options:

- **Exclude the Start In or drawing folders (recommended)**

- **Include the Start In and drawing folders**

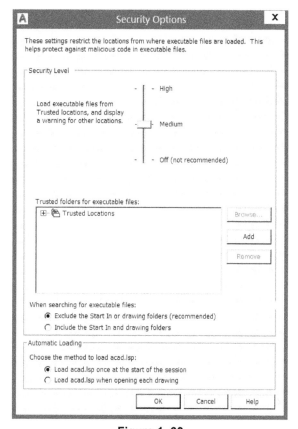

Figure 1–63

These controls or similar controls can also be found in the CAD Manager Control Utility and Deployment Wizard or by using the new system variable **LegacyCodeSearch**.

Practice 1c | Improved Graphics

Practice Objective

- Explore the AutoCAD graphical performance commands.

Estimated time for completion: 10 minutes

In this practice, you will use AutoCAD commands that highlight the graphics performance of the software.

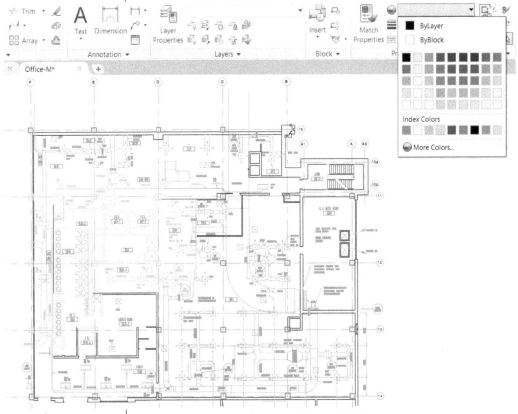

Figure 1–64

Task 1 - Change properties of multiple objects.

1. Open the **Office-M.dwg** from the practice files.

2. Using a window, select a large number of objects in the drawing.

3. In the *Home* tab>Properties panel, select the color drop-down list, as shown in Figure 1–65. Move the cursor over the various colors. The selected objects are displayed in the model as if they have been changed.

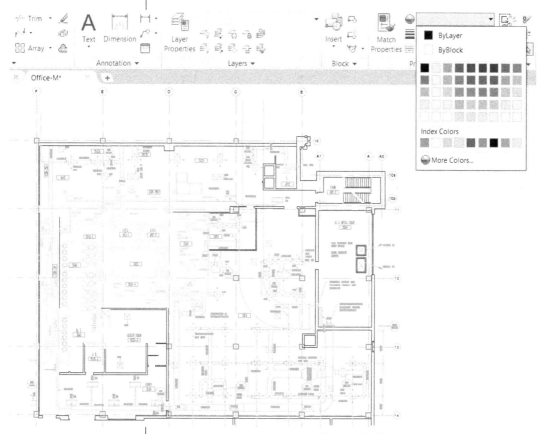

Figure 1–65

4. In the property drop-down, click on the **cyan** color to set the color for all of the objects selected.

Task 2 - Change the selection effect color.

1. Continue working in the same file as the last task.

2. Open the **Options** dialog box.

3. Click the *Selection* tab to make it active.

4. Expand the Selection effect color drop-down list and select the color red, as shown in Figure 1–66. Click **OK**.

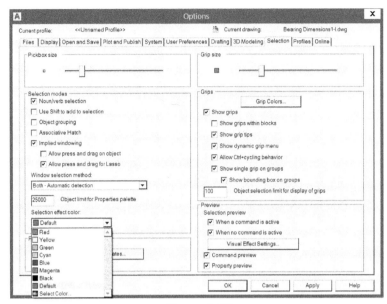

Figure 1–66

5. Start the **Move** command.

6. Select all of the objects in the model. Note that they turn red.

7. Click the basepoint near the bottom left corner of the model, as shown in Figure 1–67. Notice that you are able to move the cursor freely with the objects attached to it without waiting for the model to regen each time the cursor moves.

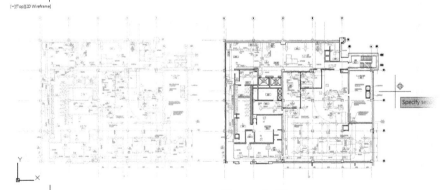

Figure 1–67

8. Press <Esc> to cancel the command.

9. Close the drawing without saving.

Chapter Review Questions

1. How do you view the updates and patches that are available for the Autodesk software that is installed on your computer?

   a. Options dialog box>*System* tab.

   b. On the status bar, right-click on ● (Hardware acceleration) and select **Graphics Performance...**.

   c. Open the Autodesk Desktop Application from the Windows desktop or on the Windows taskbar.

   d. In the Infocenter, expand the login option and select **Manage License**.

2. How would you close all the drawing files except for one which is not the active drawing file?

   a. At the top of the drawing window, right-click on the drawing tab you want to keep open and select **Close All Other**.

   b. At the command line, type **CLOSEALLOTHER**.

   c. In the application menu, right-click on the drawing you want to keep open and select **Close All Other**.

   d. Drawings can only be closed one at a time.

3. How do you toggle gallery previews off in the Ribbon?

   a. Right-click on the Ribbon and select **Turn off gallery previews**.

   b. Type **GALLERYVIEW** at the command line and set the variable to 0 (zero).

   c. They cannot be toggled off.

4. Layout tabs can be easily moved to a new location by scrolling through hidden tabs at the bottom of the drawing window.

   a. True

   b. False

5. What happens to the original objects when rotating, scaling, or stretching objects?

   a. They disappear from the drawing once you finish selecting objects.

   b. They become a dashed linetype to indicate they have been selected.

   c. They turn gray until you commit to the changes, then they disappear.

   d. Nothing. They remain as they are until the command is compete, then they disappear.

6. How do you improve the graphics performance for capable devices?

   a. Type **Graphics Performance** in the command line to change the variable.

   b. Right-click in the drawing and select **Graphics Performance**.

   c. On the *View* tab>Interface panel, click **Graphics Performance**.

   d. In the **Options** dialog box, *System* tab, click the **Graphics Performance** button.

Command Summary

Button	Command	Location
	Blend Curves	• **Ribbon:** *Home* tab>Modify panel>expand Fillet • **Command Prompt:** Blend
	Close	• **Application Menu** • **Drawing Window:** *File* tab>Shortcut menu • **Command Prompt:** Close
N/A	**Close All**	• **Drawing Window:** *File* tab>Shortcut menu • **Command Prompt:** CloseAll
N/A	**Close All Other**	• **Drawing Window:** *File* tab>Shortcut menu • **Command Prompt:** CloseAllOther
N/A	**Cursor Badge**	• **Command Prompt:** CursorBadge
	Erase	• **Ribbon:** *Home* tab>Modify panel • **Command Prompt:** Erase or E
N/A	**Gallery View**	• **Command Prompt:** GALLERYVIEW
	Hardware Acceleration	• **Status Bar**
	Isolate Objects	• **Status Bar** • **Drawing Window:** Shortcut menu • **Command Prompt:** IsolateObjects
	Lock UI	• **Status Bar** • **Command Prompt:** LOCKUI
	Rotate	• **Ribbon:** *Home* tab>Modify panel • **Command Prompt:** Rotate or RO
	Scale	• **Ribbon:** *Home* tab>Modify panel • **Command Prompt:** Scale or SC
	Stretch	• **Ribbon:** *Home* tab>Modify panel • **Command Prompt:** Stretch or S
N/A	**System Variable Monitor**	• **Command Prompt:** SysVarMonitor

Drawing Documentation

In this chapter you learn about updates and enhancements to various annotation tools. You learn how to place linear, aligned, radial, and angular dimensions, and how to add continuous and baseline dimensions. You also learn to edit dimensions, select a dimension style, and to place leaders. Then you learn how to create revision clouds and how to add text frames to Mtext objects. Finally, you learn how to create PDF files for communicating the design to others.

Learning Objectives in this Chapter

- Add linear, angular, and radial dimensions to a drawing.
- Edit dimensions grips, text, and placement location of existing dimensions.
- Annotate a drawing to include additional text and revision clouds.
- Import and export PDF Files.

2.1 Dimensioning Concepts

The AutoCAD® dimensioning commands create dimensions based on points that you specify or by selecting the object for dimensioning. The AutoCAD software automatically draws the dimension with the appropriate extension lines, arrowheads, dimension lines, and text, as shown in Figure 2–1.

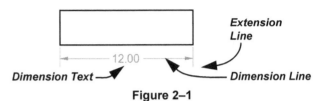

Figure 2–1

- Dimensions recalculate automatically when the objects that they refer to are modified. For example, when you stretch a wall 2'-0" to the right, the associated dimensions update.

As you prepare to dimension, you should:

- Set up a viewport in a layout that displays the part of the model that you want to dimension. You should set the Viewport Scale before you start dimensioning.

- Select the layer for dimensioning.

- Select a Dimension Style to be used for dimensioning.

Lock the viewport to make it easier to zoom around the drawing without changing the scale by mistake.

Dimension styles can be annotative.

Some dimensioning commands can also be accessed in the Home tab>Annotation panel.

- Use the *Annotate* tab>Dimensions panel, as shown in Figure 2–2, to access the dimensioning commands and set up the layer and dimension style.

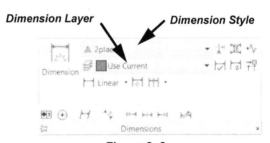

Figure 2–2

General Dimensioning

Dimensions can be added using a general dimension command or using commands specific to the type of dimension being added. The general dimension command automatically determines the type of dimension required based on the object or point selected.

- You can use a single **Dimension** command to add various dimensions, such as linear (horizontal, vertical), aligned, angular, radial etc. After placing a required dimension, the **Dimension** command remains active, enabling you to add other dimensions as required, without re-launching the command.

How To: Add Dimensions

Instead of selecting an object for dimension, you can use object snaps to snap to points to be dimensioned.

1. In the *Annotate* tab>Dimensions panel, click (Dimension).
2. Hover the cursor on the object that you want to dimension. Depending on the object that touches the cursor, a preview of a relevant dimension displays, as shown in Figure 2–3.

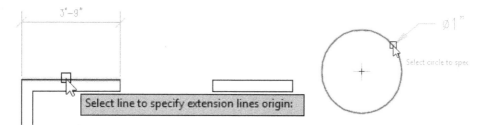

Figure 2–3

3. If the preview dimension is the correct one, click to save the dimension.
4. Drag the cursor to the location where you want the dimension to be located. Click to place the dimension or select an option from the command line (or use the <Down Arrow> menu).
5. Dimension another object in the drawing or press <Esc> to exit the command.

2.2 Adding Linear Dimensions

Linear dimensions measure a distance from one point to another, as shown in Figure 2–4.

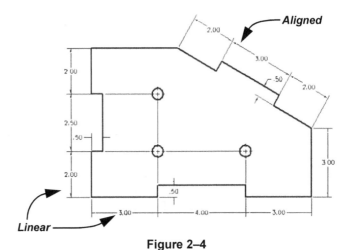

Figure 2–4

Individual Linear Dimensions

Linear dimensions can be horizontal or vertical, as shown in Figure 2–4. Aligned dimensions are also linear dimensions, however, they measure the linear distance parallel to the selected line or the selected points. The dimension line is placed parallel to the line between the two points, as shown in Figure 2–4.

*   The AutoCAD software determines the linear orientation (horizontal, vertical, or aligned) based on the selected object or where you select the point for the dimension line location.

How To: Add Linear and Aligned Dimensions

You can add dimensions in two different ways:

1. In the *Annotate* tab>Dimensions panel, click ⬚ (Dimension).
2. Select a line in the drawing.
3. Select a point to place the dimension line.

or

1. In the *Annotate* tab>Dimensions panel, click ⬚ (Dimension).
2. Select a point for the first extension line origin.
3. Select a point for the second extension line origin.
4. Select a point to place the dimension line.

Use Object Snaps to select the exact points for the extension line origins.

Hint: Oblique Extension Lines

If you want the extension lines of a linear dimension to be at an

angle, you can click ⊢⊣ (Oblique) in the *Annotate* tab> expanded Dimensions panel, to angle the lines.

Adding a Break in a Linear or Aligned Dimension

In some cases, you need to have a dimension with a break because the length of the dimension is too long to display on a sheet, as shown in Figure 2–5.

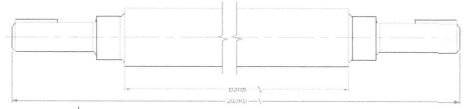

Figure 2–5

How To: Create a Jogged Linear Dimension

1. In the *Annotate* tab>Dimensions panel, click ⁺∿ (Dimjogline).
2. Select the dimension to which you want to add the jog.
3. Specify the jog location along the dimension or press <Enter> to accept the default location.

• You can remove a jog line using the command's **Remove** option.

Multiple Linear Dimensions

After you have placed a linear, aligned, or angular dimension, you can use that dimension as the beginning of a series of

related dimensions by clicking ⊢⊤⊣ (Continue) or ⊢⊣ (Baseline), as shown in Figure 2–6.

These commands can be used with Linear, Aligned, or Angular dimensions.

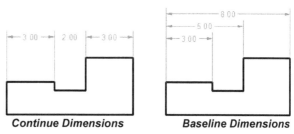

Continue Dimensions   Baseline Dimensions

Figure 2–6

Continue dimensions use the last extension line placed as the first extension line for the next dimension. The dimension line remains at the same distance from the object.

Baseline dimensions use the first extension line as the base for all other dimensions. As you select additional extension line points, the new dimension is placed over the previous one. The distance between the dimension lines is set by the dimension style.

How To: Add Continue and Baseline Dimensions

1. Place a linear or aligned dimension.
2. In the *Annotate* tab>Dimensions panel, click ⊢⊤⊣ (Continue) or ⊢→ (Baseline).
3. Select a point for the second extension line origin. The first extension line origin is automatically assumed to be from the last dimension you placed.
4. Continue selecting points for additional extension line origins.
5. Press <Enter> twice to finish the command.

- By default, the AutoCAD software uses the last dimension placed as the starting dimension. Use the **Select** option to select a different dimension to be referenced.

Quick Dimensioning

In some cases, you can place all of your dimensions along one edge of an object using one command, regardless of whether it is **Linear**, **Aligned**, **Baseline**, or **Continue**. As shown in Figure 2–7, the outside lines of the walls were selected using the **Quick Dimension** command and dimensioned at the same time.

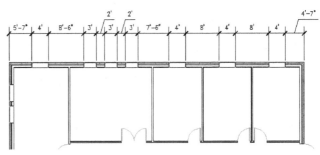

Figure 2–7

How To: Add Quick Dimensions

Quick Dimension does not enable you to place a type of dimension that is not appropriate for the selection. For example, if you select a line, you cannot place a Radius or Diameter dimension on that line.

1. In the *Annotate* tab>Dimensions panel, click ⊢⇥⊣ (Quick Dimension).
2. Select the objects that you want to dimension. When you have finished selecting objects, press <Enter>.
3. Specify the dimension line position.

- By default, the AutoCAD software creates continuous dimensions if you select linear objects or more than one object.

- You can switch between a number of other types of dimensions, including **Staggered**, **Baseline**, and **Ordinate**, in the Command Prompt, shortcut menu, or dynamic input drop-down list.

- Baseline and Ordinate dimensions start from a common point. You can set that point using the **datumPoint** option.

- There is also an **Edit** option that enables you to add or remove points. However, it is easier to do this using other commands.

Practice 2a

Adding Linear Dimensions (Architectural)

Practice Objective

* Add dimensions using various dimensioning techniques.

Estimated time for completion: 10 minutes

In this practice you will start to add dimensions using the general **Dimension** command. You will then dimension different portions of the architectural drawing using **Quick**, **Baseline**, and **Continue** dimensions, as shown in Figure 2–8.

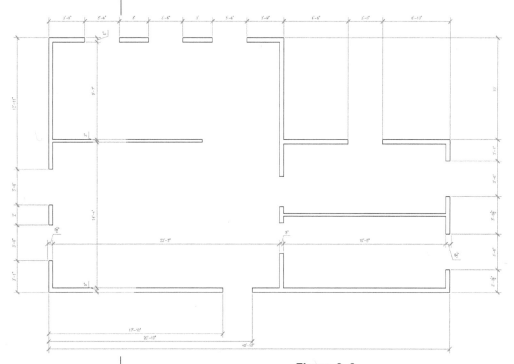

Figure 2–8

1. Open **Dimensioned Plan-A.dwg** from your practice files folder.

2. Switch to the **D-sized** layout. Make the existing viewport active and zoom extents.

3. In the Status Bar, set the *Viewport Scale* to **1/2"=1'-0"** and lock the viewport.

4. In the *Annotate* tab>Dimensions panel, select the layer **Dimensions** in the drop-down list, as shown in Figure 2–9, to make it the active dimensioning layer.

*Verify that the active Dimension Style is set as **Architectural**. This is an annotative style.*

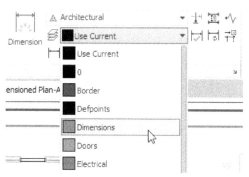

Figure 2–9

5. Freeze the layers **Doors** and **Windows** to make it easier to only select the walls to be dimensioned.

6. Verify that **Object Snap** is toggled off.

7. While still active in the viewport, in the *Annotate* tab> Dimensions panel, click (Dimension). Hover the cursor on the top left wall, as shown in Figure 2–10.

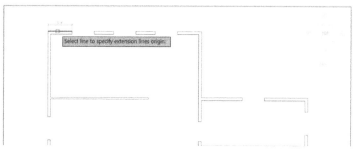

Figure 2–10

8. Select the object, drag the cursor up and click to place the dimension outside the building.

9. In the Status Bar, toggle on **Object Snap** and verify that **Endpoint** object snap is selected.

10. Start the **Continue** command. Note that the cursor is attached with the last dimension you placed. Select the left endpoint of the second wall, as shown in Figure 2–11.

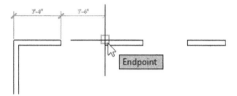

Figure 2–11

11. Select the rest of the dimension points along the same wall. Press <Enter> twice to complete the command.

The order of selection of points determines the start point of the baseline.

12. Start the **Dimension** command. Select the two endpoints (first left and then right) of the bottom left wall. Place the dimension along the bottom side of the building.

13. Start the **Baseline** command and note that the cursor dimension is attached to the left extension line of the dimension.

14. Select the left endpoint of the right side bottom wall to place the dimension.

15. Select the right endpoint of the right side bottom wall to place the third dimension. Press <Enter> twice to complete the command.

16. Start the **Quick Dimension** command.

17. Add dimensions to the left side of the building by selecting three outside wall objects.

18. If time permits, add dimensions to the right exterior of the building, and the interior.

19. Save and close the drawing.

Practice 2b

Adding Linear Dimensions (Mechanical)

Practice Objective

- Add linear dimensions to a mechanical drawing.

In this practice you will add linear and aligned dimensions to a mechanical drawing.

Estimated time for completion: 5 minutes

Task 1 - Add linear dimensions.

1. Open **Bearing Dimensions-I.dwg** from your practice files folder.

2. Switch to the **C-Sized** layout. Create two viewports (*Layout* tab>Layout Viewports panel>**Rectangular**).

*If a single viewport already exists, resize it to make room for the second viewport and verify that both viewports are in the layer **Viewports**. Leave empty space (as shown in Figure 2–12) for adding the dimensions.*

3. Zoom to display the views similar to those shown in Figure 2–12, and set the *scales* to **1:1** (left viewport) and **2:1** (right viewport). Lock the viewports.

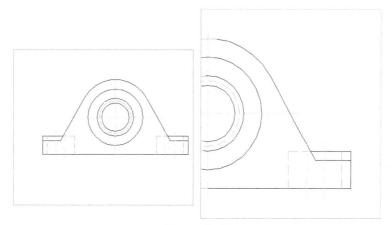

Figure 2–12

4. Make the **1:1** viewport active.

5. Change the active layer to **Dimensions** (*Annotate* tab>Dimensions panel, layer **Dimensions**).

6. Set the active *Dimension Style* to **2places**. This is an annotative style, as shown in Figure 2–13.

Figure 2–13

When you drag the cursor left, an aligned dimension might display. Drag the cursor downwards to force the display of a vertical dimension instead.

7. Start the **Dimension** command. Select the bottom left endpoint and then select the left endpoint of the green horizontal center line. Drag the cursor left and down until a vertical dimension is displayed, as shown on the right in Figure 2–14. Click to place the dimension.

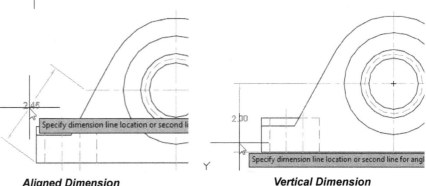

Aligned Dimension   **Vertical Dimension**

Figure 2–14

8. Still in the **Dimension** command, add the remaining vertical and horizontal dimensions shown in Figure 2–15. After placing all of the dimensions, exit the command.

*Start the **Dimension** command once, select the relevant endpoints and place the dimension for each vertical and horizontal dimension using the same command. You do not have to exit or relaunch the **Dimension** command after placing each dimension.*

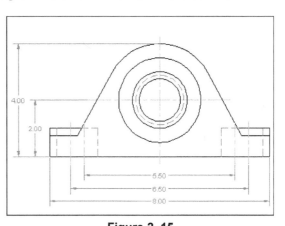

Figure 2–15

9. If required, unlock the viewport and pan to fit the dimensions into the available space. Be careful not to change the scale while the viewport is unlocked. Lock the viewport, if required, when you are finished.

Task 2 - Add aligned dimensions.

1. Make the **2:1** viewport active.

2. Start the **Dimension** command and add the vertical dimension shown in Figure 2–16.

3. Still in the **Dimension** command, select the two endpoints of the aligned line on the right side and add the aligned dimension as shown in Figure 2–16. Exit the command.

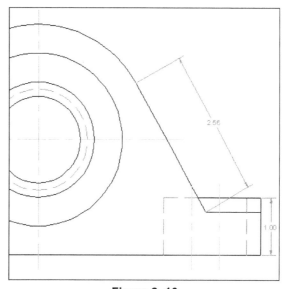

Figure 2–16

4. Save and close the drawing.

2.3 Adding Radial and Angular Dimensions

Other types of dimensions include Radius, Diameter, and Angular dimensions. Radius/Diameter dimensions for arcs and circles are placed with a leader from the object. You can also create a Jogged Radial dimension for arcs whose center point would be outside the drawing and for dimensioning the length around the curve of an arc. Angular dimensions measure the angle of an arc or the angle between two objects.

Radius and Diameter Dimensions

Radius is typically used on arcs, while **Diameter** is normally used on full circles, as shown in Figure 2–17. You can also add a radius dimension for a circle.

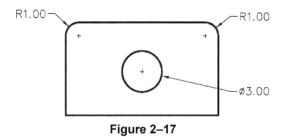

Figure 2–17

How To: Add Radius or Diameter Dimensions

1. In the *Annotate* tab>Dimensions panel, click (Dimension).
2. Select a point on the rim of an arc or circle. (You do not need to use Object Snaps for this.)
3. Select a location along the arc or circle for the dimension line text.

- When you are dimensioning a radius, you can place the dimension beyond the arc. The AutoCAD software creates an additional arc extension line as required.

- **Quick Dimension** creates a radial dimension by default if you select an arc or circular object. However, you can select **Diameter** in the options.

Associative Center Marks and Centerlines

There are two new tools which indicate the center of a arc or circle regardless of the objects' perspective. Both tools are on the *Annotate* tab>Centerlines panel.

- The ⊕ Center Mark tool adds an associate center mark at the center of selected circles, arcs, or polygonal arcs, as shown in Figure 2–18.

- The ⟋⟋ Centerline tool creates centerline geometry that is associated with selected lines and polylines, as shown in Figure 2–19.

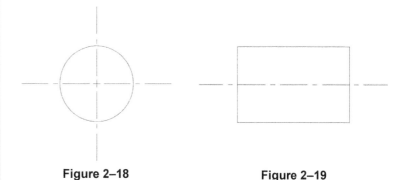

Figure 2–18   Figure 2–19

- If the associated objects move, the centerlines and center marks also update.

When a center mark or centerline is selected, grips display that enable you to control the extension line lengths, as shown in Figure 2–20. The appearance of center marks and centerlines is controlled by multiple system variables. Figure 2–20 and the table below lists the controlling variables and describes their effects.

CENTEREXE	• Sets the length of the extension line overshoots for centerlines and center marks.
CENTERMARKEXE	• Determines whether extension lines are created for center marks.
CENTERLAYER	• Sets the layer on which the centerlines and center marks are created.
CENTERLTYPE	• Sets the linetype used by centerlines and center marks.
CENTERLTSCALE	• Sets the linetype scale used by centerlines and center marks.
CENTERCROSSSIZE	• Sets the size of the central cross for center marks.
CENTERCROSSGAP	• Sets the extension line gap between the central cross and the extension lines in center marks.

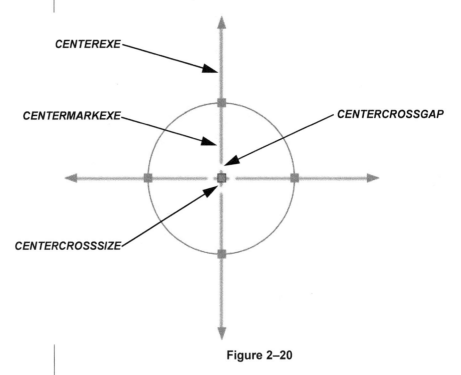

Figure 2–20

- The system variables shown in Figure 2–20 must be set prior to creating the center mark or centerline for the variable to take effect.

- CENTERRESET can be used to reset the extension lines of center marks and center line objects to the current value of CENTEREXE.

- The Properties palette can be used to modify select attributes, as shown in Figure 2–21.

- A multi-functional grip menu offers additional controls, as shown in Figure 2–22.

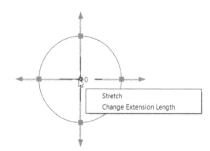

Figure 2–21   Figure 2–22

Jogged Radial Dimension

If the center mark of the circle or arc you are dimensioning does not display in the view, you can use the **Jogged** command to create an override for the center, as shown in Figure 2–23.

Figure 2–23

How To: Create a Jogged Radial Dimension

1. In the *Annotate* tab>Dimensions panel, click ⌐ (Jogged).
2. Select the arc or circle that you want to dimension.
3. Specify a point for the center location override.
4. Specify the dimension line location. This also sets the location of the text.
5. Specify the jog location.

Arc Length Dimension

The arc length describes the distance from one end point of an arc to the other end point along the curve of the arc, as shown in Figure 2–24. This command can be used to dimension individual arcs or arcs that are parts of polylines.

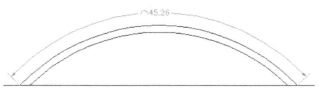

Figure 2–24

How To: Dimension the Arc Length

1. In the *Annotate* tab>Dimensions panel, click ▢ (Dimension).
2. Hover the cursor over the arc that you want to dimension.
3. Press <Down Arrow> and select **Arc Length** from the list.
4. Specify the dimension location.

Angular Dimensions

You can add angular dimensions to lines, circles, and arcs and from a vertex, as shown in Figure 2–25.

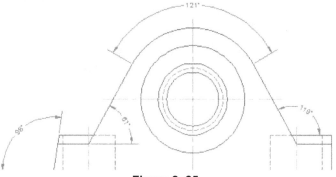

Figure 2–25

- When you are placing the Angular dimension, you can place it at any of the four quadrants of the angle.

How To: Add Angular Dimensions

1. In the *Annotate* tab>Dimensions panel, click 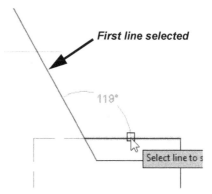 (Dimension).
2. Select a line, arc, or circle.
3. If you select a **line**, you are prompted to place a linear dimension. As you hover the cursor over another line, the preview changes to an angle dimension, as shown in Figure 2–26. Select the second line and specify the location of the dimension line.

First line selected

119°

Select line to s

Figure 2–26

4. If you hover over an **arc**, by default you can place a radial dimension. Press <Down Arrow> and select **Angular**. Then, click the arc to select it. Click again to set the location of the dimension line.
5. If you hover over a **circle**, by default you can place a diameter dimension. Press <Down Arrow> and select **Angular**. Then click the circle to select it. Click to specify the first side of the angle. Click again to set the second side of the angle. Click one more time to set the location of the dimension line.

• You can also dimension an angle from a vertex. Before selecting an object, press <Enter> and use Object Snaps to select an angle vertex. Specify the first and second angle end points and place the dimension line.

Practice 2c

Adding Radial and Angular Dimensions (Architectural)

Practice Objective

Estimated time for completion: 5 minutes

- Add dimensions including radial and angular to a drawing.

In this practice you will add Angular, Radial, Diameter, Aligned, and Arc Length dimensions, as shown in Figure 2–27.

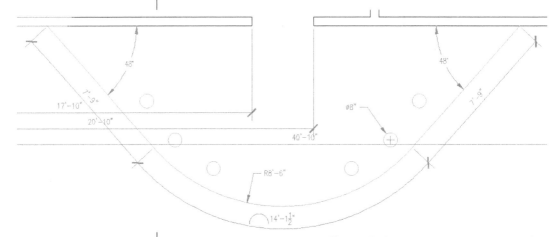

Figure 2–27

1. Open **Dimensioned Plan1-A.dwg** from your practice files folder.

2. In the Layer Control, toggle on the layer **Misc** to display the entrance portico.

3. Modify the viewport to display the entire entrance portico. If the viewport is locked, unlock it and pan the view until it fits. Zooming in and out of the view changes the viewport scale. Verify that the *Viewport Scale* is set at **1/2"=1'-0"**. Lock the viewport when you are finished. You can also change the size of the viewport if it is too small.

4. Activate the viewport. Verify that the layer **Dimensions** is active.

5. In the *Annotate* tab>Dimensions panel, verify that the dimension layer is set to **Use Current**.

6. In the *Annotate* tab>Dimensions panel, click ⬓ (Dimension).

7. Hover the cursor over one of the six circled columns. If the cursor does not display the diameter dimension (while hovering over the circle), toggle off **Object Snap** in the Status Bar. Select the circle to accept the diameter dimension and click again to place it at the required location.

8. Still in the **Dimension** command, hover the cursor over the arc of the portico. It displays the radial dimension.

9. Press <Down Arrow> and select **arc Length**, as shown in Figure 2–28.

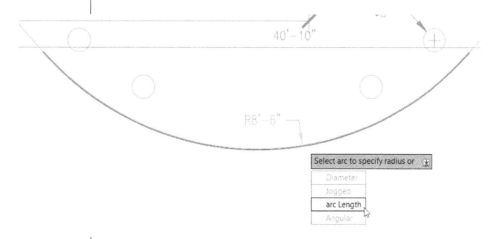

Figure 2–28

10. Select the arc and click again to place the dimension outside the arc, as shown in Figure 2–27.

11. Still in the **Dimension** command, hover the cursor over the arc of the portico again. Press <Down Arrow> and select **Radius**. Select the arc and click again to place the radius dimension on the inside of the portico arc.

12. Toggle on **Object Snap** in the Status Bar.

13. Still in the **Dimension** command, select the two endpoints of the angled line that joins the portico arc with the building wall. Add Aligned dimension to both the angled lines. (Use the end of the arc length dimension line to keep the connected dimensions in line.)

14. Still in the **Dimension** command, select one of the angled line again. Hover the cursor over the wall line that touches the selected angled line to display the angled dimension, as shown in Figure 2–29.

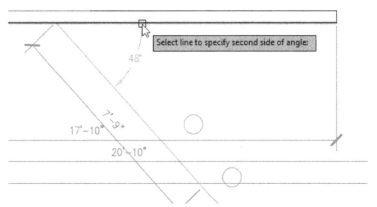

Figure 2–29

15. Select the line to accept the angled dimension and click again to place it, as shown in Figure 2–27.

16. Add **Angular** dimensions on the other side as well.

17. Save and close the drawing.

Practice 2d

Adding Radial and Angular Dimensions (Mechanical)

Practice Objective

- Add radial, diameter, and angular dimensions to a drawing.

Estimated time for completion: 5 minutes

In this practice you will add Center Mark, Radius, Diameter, and Angular dimensions to a mechanical drawing, as shown in Figure 2–30.

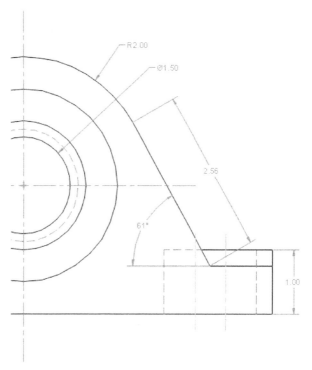

Figure 2–30

1. Open **Bearing Dimensions1-I.dwg** from your practice files folder.

2. Activate the **2:1** (right side) viewport.

3. In the *Annotate* tab>Dimensions panel, set the dimension layer to **Dimensions**.

4. Using the **Center Mark** command, add a center mark with extension lines to the center circle.

5. Using the **Dimension** command, add a **Radius** dimension to the arc at the top of the bearing.

6. At the command line, type **CENTEREXE**. Type **2** for the value.

7. At the command line, type **CENTERRESET**.

8. Select the center mark and press <Enter>.

9. Add a **Diameter** dimension to the innermost circle.

10. Add an **Angular** dimension to the angle of the sloped line. (Select the horizontal line first and then hover on the sloped line.)

11. Save and close the drawing.

2.4 Editing Dimensions

If the dimensions are interfering with other parts in a drawing, as shown in Figure 2–31, you can edit and modify them using grips and special tools in the shortcut menu. You can also edit the dimension text. Additional tools available to clean up dimensions include aligning dimensions and breaking extension lines.

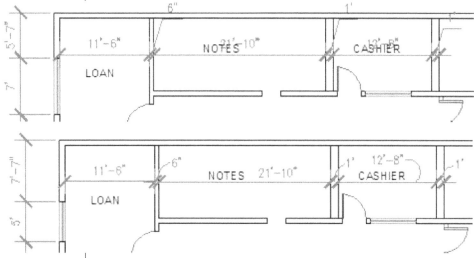

Figure 2–31

- The AutoCAD dimensions are associative. Therefore, when you change a dimensioned object, the dimensions update to reflect the change. If you move an object, the dimensions move as well. If you change the size of an object, the dimensions display the change.

- To change the dimension style of an existing dimension, select it and then set the appropriate dimension style in the Dimension Style drop-down list, in the *Annotate* tab> Dimensions panel.

Dimension Shortcut Menu

You can select a dimension or multiple dimensions, and then right-click to access additional options in the shortcut menu, as shown in Figure 2–32.

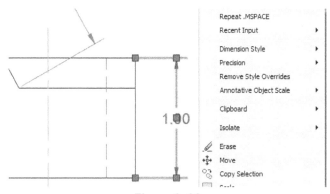

Figure 2–32

- You can change the Dimension Style of selected dimensions using the **Dimension Style** option. The dimension style controls the basic features of a dimension, such as the text location and number of decimal places.

- You can change the precision of selected dimensions using the **Precision** option. Precision helps you to display dimensions to a specific number of decimal places.

Editing Dimensions Using Grips

Grips can be used to relocate dimension elements. Without starting a command, select the following to display its grips at various parts of the dimension, as shown in Figure 2–33.

- Where extension lines touch the dimensioned object.

- Where the extension line and dimension line meet.

- On the dimension text.

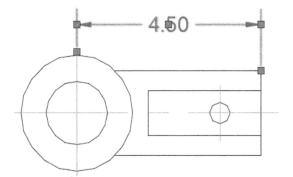

Figure 2–33

Once the dimension grips are displayed, you can edit the dimension as follows:

- Select the grip at the dimension line and move it to change the distance from the object.

- Select the grip on the text and move it to change the location of the text (and sometimes the dimension line).

- Select the grip at the extension line origin to change the length of the dimension. (This option might disconnect the associativity to the object it is dimensioning.)

- Press <Esc> to clear the grips.

Dimension Grips Shortcut Options

Additional options are available for editing dimensions using the multifunctional grips. Hover the cursor over a grip, and select an option in the dynamic input list. Depending on the specific grip you hover over, a different list of options displays, as shown in Figure 2–34.

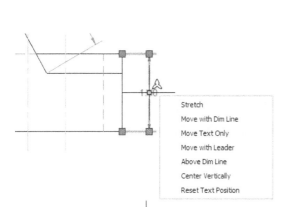
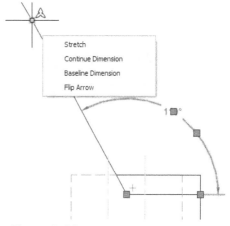

Figure 2–34

- Use the various text options, such as **Move Text Only** and **Above Dim Line** to move the text to a different position.

- **Reset Text Position** returns the moved text to its original location.

- You can use an existing dimension as the beginning of a series of related dimensions in either **Continue** or **Baseline**.

- Use **Flip Arrow** if the arrowheads on a dimension were pushed out and you want them to be inside the extension lines or on the opposite side.

- You can also access these options by selecting a grip (making it hot), and then using <Ctrl> to cycle through the options, or right-clicking and selecting one in the shortcut menu, as shown in Figure 2–35.

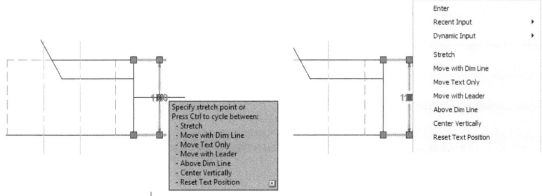

Figure 2–35

Editing the Dimension Text

Dimensions are associated with the objects they reference. However, sometimes you might need to add text to a dimension (such as +/- in renovation work), as shown in Figure 2–36.

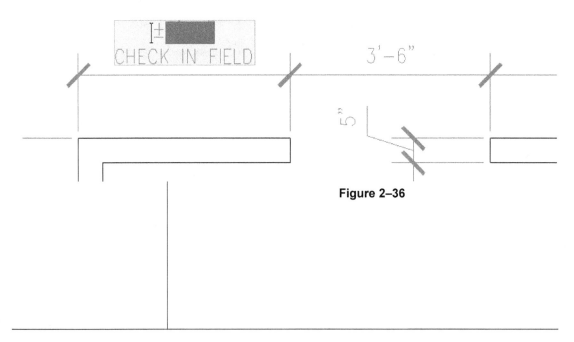

Figure 2–36

- To change the dimension text, double-click on the dimension text or type **ddedit**. The default dimension text or value is inserted as a special field in the Text Editor. You can add text before or after the field, or delete the field to completely replace the default text When editing dimension text, a width sizing control is displayed above the text. This enables you to adjust the text width for text wrapping, as shown in Figure 2–37.

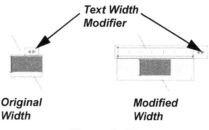

Figure 2–37

- If you remove the text associated with the dimension by mistake and want to get it back, type **<>** in the Text Editor.

Adjusting Dimension Spacing

When you create stacked angular or linear dimensions of any type, they might be too close together or unevenly spaced, as shown in Figure 2–38. Instead of moving each dimension, you can modify the space between sets of dimensions using the **Adjust Space** command.

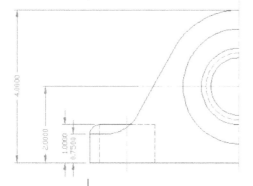 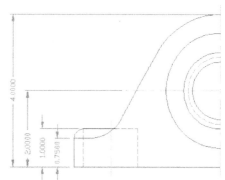

Figure 2–38

How To: Modify the Space Between Dimensions

1. In the *Annotate* tab>Dimensions panel, click ⬚ (Adjust Space).
2. Select the base dimension (the one closest to the object) of the group you want to modify.
3. Select the rest of the dimensions in the group.
4. Type the distance that you want to have between dimensions or press <Enter> to accept the automatic distance.

Dimension Breaks

When there are many dimensions in a drawing, the various extension lines and dimension lines can start to overlap. In that case, you can create dimension breaks without changing the associativity of the dimension object, as shown in Figure 2–39.

- When the object is stretched, the dimensions change and the breaks remain in place. This makes revising a drawing easier, as you do not need to re-dimension a modified part.

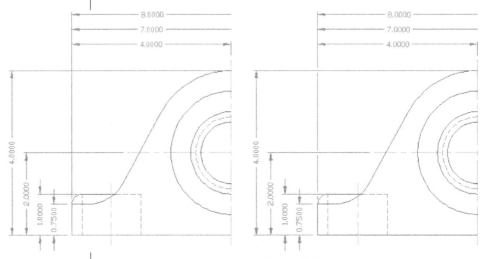

Figure 2–39

How To: Break One Dimension

1. In the *Annotate* tab>Dimensions panel, click ⊥ (Dimension Break).
2. Select a dimension to break.
3. Select an object to break the dimension or select one of the options.
4. Continue to select other objects to break their dimensions as required.
5. Press <Enter> to complete the command.

- The **Multiple** option enables you to select more than one dimension to break. The selected dimensions are broken where they overlap other dimensions.

- To remove breaks from a dimension, start the **Break** command, select the dimension, and select the **Remove** option.

Practice 2e

Editing Dimensions (Architectural)

Practice Objective

- Modify dimensions, edit dimension text, and break dimensions in a drawing.

Estimated time for completion: 10 minutes

In this practice you will modify dimensions using grips, edit the dimension text, and break dimensions using the **Dim, Break** command, as shown in Figure 2–40.

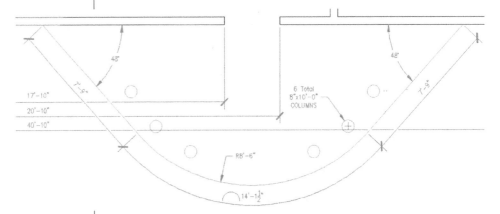

Figure 2–40

1. Open **Dimensioned Plan2-A.dwg** from your practice files folder.

2. Make the viewport active and verify that it is locked, so that you can zoom and pan as required to modify the dimensions.

3. Focusing on the portico area, use grips to move the three horizontal dimension text to the left hand side, outside of the portico area.

4. In the *Annotate* tab>Dimensions panel, click ⊥⊣ (Break) and press <Down Arrow> to open the options menu. Select **Multiple**.

5. Select the three horizontal dimensions and press <Enter>.

6. Select the green portico line. Note that the three horizontal dimension lines break where they are passing through the portico arc object.

7. Select the aligned dimension line on both sides to create a break with them as well.

8. Press <Enter> to exit the command.

You can also use the **ddedit** *command.*

9. Double-click on the diameter **Ø 8** dimension for the column and type **6 Total 8"x10'-0" COLUMNS,** as shown on the left in Figure 2–41.

10. Use ◄► to change the width for text wrapping, as shown on the right in Figure 2–41.

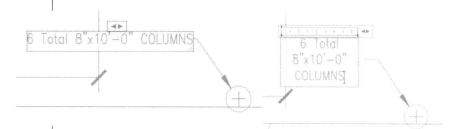

Figure 2–41

11. Save and close the drawing.

Practice 2f | Editing Dimensions (Mechanical)

Practice Objective

- Modify the text and move dimensions.

Estimated time for completion: 5 minutes

In this practice you will modify the text of several dimensions and move the dimensions as required using grips, as shown in Figure 2–42.

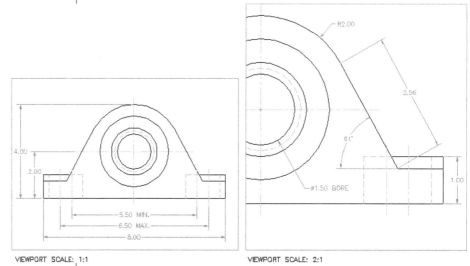

VIEWPORT SCALE: 1:1   VIEWPORT SCALE: 2:1

Figure 2–42

1. Open **Bearing Dimensions2-I.dwg** from your practice files folder.

2. Activate the **2:1** viewport and modify the text of the diameter dimension (of the innermost circle) so that it reads **Ø1.5 BORE.** Then change the width for text wrapping, as shown in Figure 2–43.

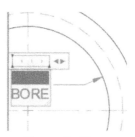

Figure 2–43

3. In the **1:1** viewport, modify the text of the two horizontal dimensions, as shown in Figure 2–44.

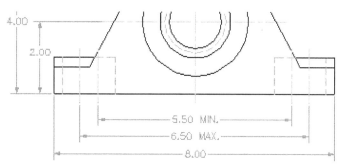

Figure 2–44

4. Use grips to move any of the other dimensions as required to a location where they are easier to read. You can also use the **Adjust Space** command to even out the bottom dimensions as required.

5. Save and close the drawing.

2.5 Other Annotations

Text

The Properties palette is useful for changing multiple instances of text. You can change general properties (such as the layer) or specific properties (such as style, height, or justification). Now you can also add a text frame around multi-line text, as shown in Figure 2–45.

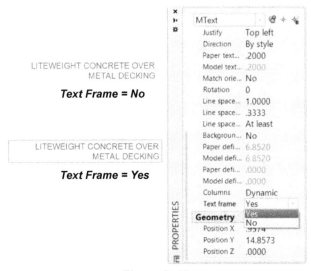

Figure 2–45

Hint: Frame Offset Value

The text frame is offset from the text by the value specified in the Background Mask dialog box, in the *Border offset factor* field, as shown in Figure 2–46.

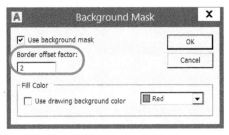

Figure 2–46

How To: Add a Text Frame

1. Select the multi-line text.
2. Right-click and select **Properties**.
3. In the Properties palette, change the *Text Frame* field to **Yes**.

Text Edit

The TEXTEDIT command includes a new option that enables you to edit multiple text objects without restarting the command, as shown in Figure 2–47. By default, the text edit mode is set to **Multiple**. This means that TEXTEDIT repeats, enabling you to continue selecting text objects for editing.

- When in Multiple mode, you can select **Undo** in the command line to undo the last text edit.

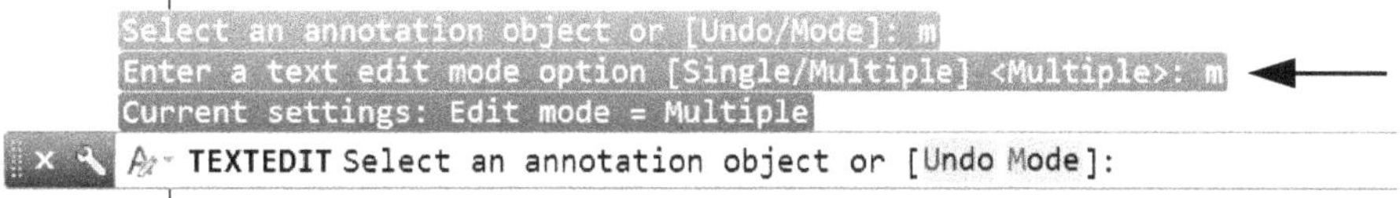

```
Select an annotation object or [Undo/Mode]: m
Enter a text edit mode option [Single/Multiple] <Multiple>: m
Current settings: Edit mode = Multiple
```
```
x    A TEXTEDIT Select an annotation object or [Undo Mode]:
```

Figure 2–47

How To: Only Edit One Text Object at a Time

1. Type **TextEdit** to start the command.
2. Select **Mode** in the command line.
3. Select **Single** in the command line.
4. Select the text to edit in the Drawing Window.

Revision Clouds

Create Revision Clouds

Revision clouds have been enhanced to provide multiple shapes for revision clouds. The most recently used creation option is used by default. The **REVCLOUDCREATEMODE** system variable can be used to set your own default creation method. Creation options now available include:

- Rectangular

- Polygonal

- Freehand

The capability of turning any object into a revision cloud is still available. Any of the Revision Cloud commands can be used for this purpose.

How To: Create a Rectangular Revision Cloud

1. In the *Annotate* tab>Markup panel, click the Revision Cloud drop-down list and select ⬚ (Rectangular).
2. In the model, click the first corner of the rectangle to start the revision cloud.
3. In the model, click the opposite corner of the rectangle to complete the revision cloud.

How To: Create a Polygonal Revision Cloud

1. In the *Annotate* tab>Markup panel, click the Revision Cloud drop-down list and select ⬚ (Polygonal).
2. In the model, click the first point of the polygon to start the revision cloud.
3. In the model, click the second point of the polygon.
4. Continue clicking points as required.
5. Press <Enter> to complete the revision cloud.

How To: Create a Freehand Revision Cloud

1. In the *Annotate* tab>Markup panel, click the Revision Cloud drop-down list and select ⬚ (Freehand).
2. In the model, click to start the revision cloud.
3. Move the mouse freely to draw the revision cloud.
4. Move the mouse close to the beginning point to complete the revision cloud. It should automatically close itself.

   Alternatively, if you prefer to have an open revision cloud, left click the end point and press <Enter> to end the command without closing the revision cloud object.

How To: Create a Revision Cloud from an Object

1. In the *Annotate* tab>Markup panel, click ⬚ (Revision Cloud).
2. Select **Object** from the command line or shortcut menu.
3. In the model, select the object. A preview of the revision cloud is displayed.
4. Select **Yes** or **No** to the set direction of the revision cloud arcs and end the command.

Edit Revision Clouds

Revision Cloud editing has been enhanced by reducing the number of grips available. If a revision cloud is created from an object, the grips for the original object display. If it is created using the rectangular or polygonal methods, grips are displayed at each vertex and at the midpoint of each line. Figure 2–48 shows grips for each type of revision cloud.

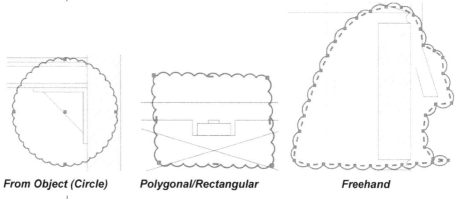

From Object (Circle)   *Polygonal/Rectangular*   *Freehand*

Figure 2–48

2.6 PDF Enhancements

Export to PDF Files

The output to PDF capability has been significantly enhanced. Certain fonts are now searchable in the PDF output files. The output control has been separated for DWF and PDF outputs, as shown in Figure 2–49. You now have access to Export to PDF options control quality, and can set hyperlinks, bookmarks, and more.

Figure 2–49

Export to PDF Options

When exporting drawing files to PDF files, you can now control the quality of vectors, rasters, and merge control (enables lines to merge or overwrite each other), as shown in Figure 2–50. You can also include information about data, such as:

- **Layer information**: Layer information can now be included in PDF files.
- **Hyperlinks**: Hyperlinks in the drawing file now work inside the PDF file. This works for sheets that are linked and for weblinks.
- **Bookmarks**: Bookmarks are now enabled. Each sheet and each sheet view becomes a bookmark in the PDF.
- **Fonts**: If you have a PDF file with shx fonts, they display as common in the PDF file. You can also covert all text to geometry during the export process.

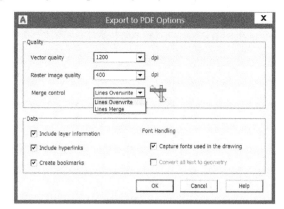

Figure 2–50

Additional PDF options are available from the printer drop-down list, which provides various print qualities, as shown in Figure 2–51. The table below lists the output settings for each PDF printer.

Printer/Plotter	Vector Quality	Raster Image Quality	Merge Control	Include Layer Info.	Include Hyperlinks	Create Bookmarks	Capture fonts used in the drawing
General Documentation	1200	400	Lines Overwrite	X	X	X	X
High Quality	2400	600	Lines Overwrite	X	X	X	X
Small Files	200	400	Lines Overwrite				
Web and Mobile	200	400	Lines Overwrite	X	X	X	X

Note that the **Convert all text to geometry** command is not available for any of the default PDF printers.

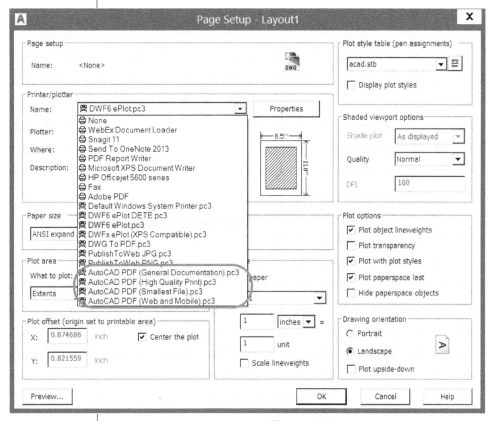

Figure 2–51

Import from PDF Files

The Import tool has been enhanced enable you to import geometry, TrueType text, and raster images from PDF files. When geometry is imported from a PDF, it is converted into AutoCAD objects in the current drawing.

How To: Import PDF Files

1. On the *Insert* Tab>Import panel, click (PDF Import).
2. When prompted, select an attached PDF file. To select an external PDF file, click **File** in the command line.
   - If you select an attached PDF file, you can set a clipping boundary. Once selected, you can choose to keep the PDF file attached, detach it, or unload it.
   - If you click **File**, the Select PDF File dialog box opens, as shown in Figure 2–52. Select the PDF you want to import and click **Open**.

If you select an attached PDF file, you cannot select which options to use when converting PDF objects into AutoCAD geometry.

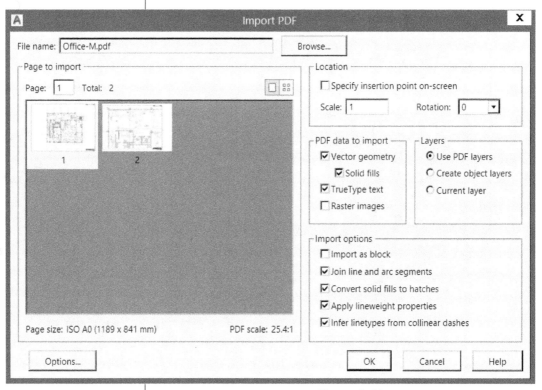

Figure 2–52

3. In the Import PDF dialog box, set the following options:

- In the *Page to Import* area, select which page of the PDF file to import.

- In the *Location* area, specify the insertion point, *Scale*, and *Rotation* of the imported geometry.

- In the *PDF data to import* area, select the types of data to import:
    - **Vector geometry**: Lines that touch become connected polylines.
    - **Solid fills**: Joins 2D solids with coincident edges to create hatch objects.
    - **TrueType text**: Converts TrueType fonts to text objects. (PDF files so not recognize SHX fonts. When drawings with SHX fonts are plotted to PDF, any text in a SHX font is converted to geometry.)
    - **Raster images**: Extracts images to PNG files, which are then attached to the drawing as reference files.

- In the *Layers* area, set which layers the imported objects are added to.

- In the *Import Options* area, set options that are used as geometry is imported:
    - **Import as block**: Creates a single block rather than separate lines.
    - **Join line and arc segments**: Creates polylines from connected objects.
    - **Convert solid fills to hatches**: Joins 2D solids with coincident edges to create hatch objects.
    - **Apply lineweight properties**: Assigns imported geometry a lineweight according to its thickness in the PDF.
    - **Infer linetypes from collinear dashes**: Creates a single polyline from collinear dash and dot segments. Then assigns a linetype and linetype scale according to the length of the dashes.

4. Once the options are set, click **OK**.

*Selecting **Solid fills** increases the processing time.*

The Files tab of the Options dialog box controls where extracted images are saved.

Hint: PDF Import Settings

When you select an attached PDF file, the *PDF Underlay*

contextual tab contains a new tool, ![PDF] (Import as Objects). Clicking this tool, and then clicking **Settings** in the command line provides the same settings found in the Import PDF dialog box, as shown in Figure 2–53.

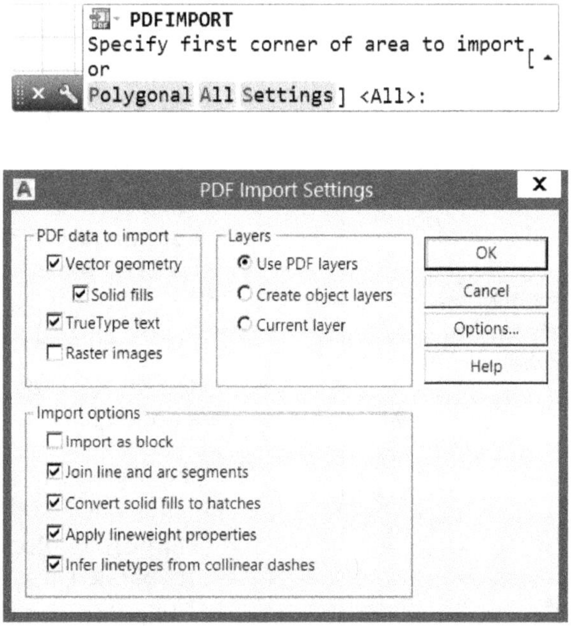

PDFIMPORT
Specify first corner of area to import
or
Polygonal All Settings] <All>:

PDF Import Settings

PDF data to import
- ☑ Vector geometry
- ☑ Solid fills
- ☑ TrueType text
- ☐ Raster images

Layers
- ◉ Use PDF layers
- ○ Create object layers
- ○ Current layer

OK
Cancel
Options...
Help

Import options
- ☐ Import as block
- ☑ Join line and arc segments
- ☑ Convert solid fills to hatches
- ☑ Apply lineweight properties
- ☑ Infer linetypes from collinear dashes

Figure 2–53

Practice 2g

Modifying Annotations

Practice Objectives

- Modify Multiline text objects using the Properties palette.
- Place revision clouds around changes in the drawing.

Estimated time for completion: 15 minutes

In this practice you will modify text using the Properties palette and place revision clouds to clearly designate changes to the drawing, as shown in Figure 2–54. Then, you will print a PDF copy of the results.

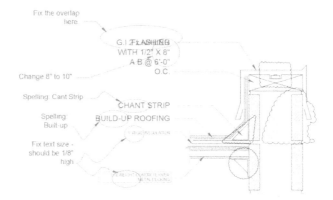

Figure 2–54

Task 1 - Edit multi-line text in a drawing.

1. Open **Detail Sheet-A.dwg** from your practice files folder.

2. Switch to the **Detail Sheet** layout if it is not already selected.

3. Zoom in on the Roof Detail in the upper left corner of the layout.

4. Double-click inside the viewport to make it active.

5. Click once on the text that is connected to the bottom leader.

6. Right-click and select **Properties**.

7. In the Properties palette, change the *Text Frame* field to **Yes**.

8. Close the Properties palette and press <Esc> to clear the text.

Task 2 - Create revision clouds.

1. Continue working in the same drawing as the last task.

2. In the *Annotate* tab>Markup panel, click the Revision Cloud drop-down list and select ⌣ (Rectangular).

3. In the model, click the first corner of the rectangle to start the revision cloud.

4. In the model, click the opposite corner of the rectangle to complete the revision cloud. Figure 2–55 shows the complete revision cloud selected.

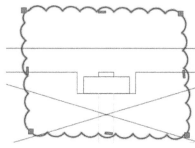

Figure 2–55

5. In the *Annotate* tab>Markup panel, click the Revision Cloud drop-down list and select ⌣ (Freehand).

6. In the model, click the first point of the polygon to start the revision cloud. Move the cursor around the triangle to create a revision cloud. Figure 2–56 shows the complete revision cloud.

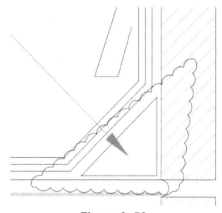

Figure 2–56

7. In the model, click the second point of the polygon.

8. Press <Enter> to complete the revision cloud.

9. If time permits, create a circle and turn it into a revision cloud. Then create a freehand revision cloud, as shown in Figure 2–57.

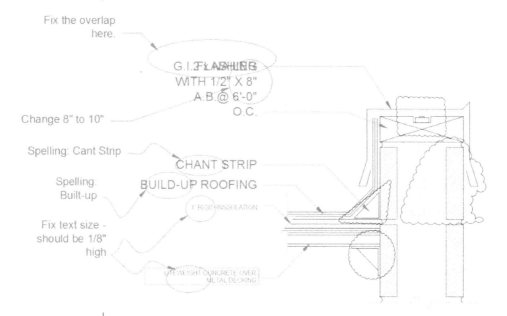

Figure 2–57

Task 3 - Print the sheet to PDF.

1. Continue working in the same drawing as the last task.

2. Go to the *Detail Sheet* layout tab.

3. Right-click on the *Detail Sheet* layout tab, select **Page Setup Manager**.

4. In the Page Setup Manager dialog box, click **Modify**.

5. In the *Printer/plotter* area, select **AutoCAD PDF (Web and Mobile.pc3)** from the Name drop-down list, as shown in Figure 2–58. Click **OK** then **Close** to return to the drawing.

6. In the *Output* tab>Plot panel, click **Plot**.

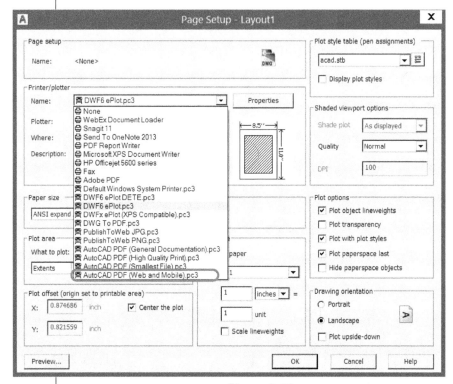

Figure 2–58

7. In the Page Setup dialog box, click **OK**.

8. In the Browse for Plot File dialog box, click **Save**. The detail sheet .PDF opens.

9. Close the drawing file without saving.

Task 4 - Import a PDF.

1. Start a new drawing: in the *Start* tab, expand **Templates** and select **acad.dwt**.

2. On the *Insert* Tab>Import panel, click (PDF Import).

3. When prompted, select an external PDF file by clicking **File** in the command line.

4. In the Select PDF File dialog box, in the *C:\AutoCAD 2017 Update Practice Files* folder, select **Office-M.pdf**. Click **Open**.

5. In the Import PDF dialog box, set the following, as shown in Figure 2–59:
    - *Page to import* area: Set *Page:* **1**
    - Clear the following three options and ensure that all of the other options are selected:
        - *Location* area: **Specify insertion point on screen**
        - *PDF data to import* area: **Raster images**
        - *Import options* area: **Import as block**
    - *Layers* area: Select **Use PDF layers**

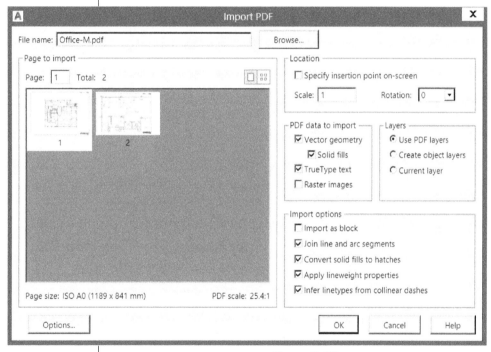

Figure 2–59

6. Click **OK**.

Chapter Review Questions

1. Which command would you use to display the length of a diagonal line so that the dimension line is parallel to the diagonal line?

   a. **Dimension**

   b. **Quick Dimension**

   c. **Baseline Dimension**

   d. **Adjust Space**

2. What is the purpose of **Continue Dimension**?

   a. Place a dimension at an angle.

   b. Stretch an existing dimension to a different location.

   c. Create a series of dimensions along one side of an object.

   d. Create a foreshortened dimension.

3. You can use the **ddedit** command to change the text displayed in a dimension.

   a. True

   b. False

4. How would you move a dimension so that the dimension line is farther away from the object?

   a. Use the **Move** command.

   b. Use the **Baseline Dimension** command.

   c. Use grips to stretch the dimension.

   d. Use the **Dimension Update** command.

5. Which of the following commands dimensions all of the selected objects?

   a. **Quick Dimension**

   b. **Aligned Dimension**

   c. **Linear Dimension**

   d. **Ordinate Dimension**

6. Which command do you use to clean up overlapping dimension lines?

   a. **Adjust Space**

   b. **Dimension Cleanup**

   c. **Dimension Break**

   d. **Jogged**

7. How do you add a frame to multi-line text?

   a. Draw a rectangle.

   b. In the *Text Editor* tab>Formatting panel, put a check in the Frame box.

   c. In the model, select the text, right-click and select **Properties**. In the Properties palette set the *Text Frame* field to **Yes**.

   d. Frames cannot be added to multi-line text.

8. If you create a revision cloud from a circle, how many grips should you see when you select the revision cloud?

   a. Several, it will depend on the size of the circle.

   b. 1

   c. 4

   d. 5

9. Which default PDF printer option creates PDF files with a vector quality of 2400 dpi and a raster image quality of 600 dpi?

   a. General Documentation

   b. High Quality

   c. Small Files

   d. Web and Mobile

10. What kind of text objects imported from PDF files can become text objects in the drawing file?

   a. SHX Fonts

   b. TrueType Fonts

   c. Text from PDF files is not recognized by AutoCAD

   d. Simplex

Command Summary

Button	Command	Location
	Centerline	• **Ribbon:** *Annotate* tab>Centerlines panel • **Command Prompt:** centerline
	Center Mark	• **Ribbon:** *Annotate* tab>Centerlines panel • **Command Prompt:** centermark
	Dimension	• **Ribbon:** *Annotate* tab>Dimensions panel or *Home* tab>Annotation panel • **Command Prompt:** dim
	Dimension: Adjust Space	• **Ribbon:** *Annotate* tab>Dimensions panel • **Command Prompt:** dimspace
	Dimension: Aligned	• **Ribbon:** *Home* tab>Annotation panel or *Annotate* tab>Dimensions panel • **Command Prompt:** dimaligned
	Dimension: Angular	• **Ribbon:** *Home* tab>Annotation panel or *Annotate* tab>Dimensions panel • **Command Prompt:** dimangular
	Dimension: Arc Length	• **Ribbon:** *Home* tab>Annotation panel or *Annotate* tab>Dimensions panel • **Command Prompt:** dimarc
	Dimension: Baseline	• **Ribbon:** *Annotate* tab>Dimensions panel • **Command Prompt:** dimbaseline
	Dimension: Break	• **Ribbon:** *Annotate* tab>Dimensions panel • **Command Prompt:** dimbreak
	Dimension: Center Mark	• **Ribbon:** *Annotate* tab>expanded Dimensions panel • **Command Prompt:** dimcenter
	Dimension: Continue	• **Ribbon:** *Annotate* tab>Dimensions panel • **Command Prompt:** dimcontinue
	Dimension: Diameter	• **Ribbon:** *Home* tab>Annotation panel or *Annotate* tab>Dimensions panel • **Command Prompt:** dimdiameter
	Dimension, Dimjogline	• **Ribbon:** *Home* tab>Annotation panel or *Annotate* tab>Dimensions panel • **Command Prompt:** dimjogline
N/A	**Dimension: Edit Text**	• **Command Prompt:** ddedit
	Dimension: Jogged (Radial)	• **Ribbon:** *Home* tab>Annotation panel or *Annotate* tab>Dimensions panel • **Command Prompt:** dimjogged
	Dimension: Linear	• **Ribbon:** *Home* tab>Annotation panel or *Annotate* tab>Dimensions panel • **Command Prompt:** dimlinear

	Dimension: Radius	• **Ribbon:** *Home* tab>Annotation panel or *Annotate* tab>Dimensions panel • **Command Prompt:** dimradius
	Freehand Revision Cloud	• **Ribbon:** *Annotate* tab>Markup panel • **Command Prompt:** revcloud
	Oblique	• **Ribbon:** *Annotate* tab>expanded Dimensions panel
	PDF Import	• **Ribbon:** *Insert* tab>Import panel • **Command Prompt:** pdfimport
	Polygonal Revision Cloud	• **Ribbon:** *Annotate* tab>Markup panel • **Command Prompt:** revcloud
	Quick Dimension	• **Ribbon:** *Annotate* tab>Dimensions panel • **Command Prompt:** qdim
	Rectangular Revision Cloud	• **Ribbon:** *Annotate* tab>Markup panel • **Command Prompt:** revcloud
N/A	**Text Edit**	• **Command Prompt:** textedit

3D Modeling

In this chapter you learn about the enhancements to 3D and the new 3D capabilities of the AutoCAD® software. You learn how to automatically create 2D documentation of existing 3D models, attach and manage point cloud data, and how to render a model.

Learning Objectives in this Chapter

- Attach and manage point clouds.
- Create a rendered image.

3.1 Point Clouds

In the *Insert* tab>Point Cloud panel, the **Create Point Cloud**

command has been replaced with (Autodesk Recap) (as shown in Figure 3–1), which launches the Autodesk Recap software in which you can import, modify, and clean up point cloud data.

Figure 3–1

The **Create Point Cloud** command has been removed from the AutoCAD software and you can no longer create files in the .PCG and .ISD file formats or import them. If you have drawings that contain point clouds in those formats they display and can be modified. The new point cloud file formats are .RCP and .RCS. They are faster and more efficient than the previous file formats and are created using the Autodesk Recap software.

- As with XREFs, images, and other externally referenced files, you can attach and manage point clouds using the External References Manager.

- Point cloud object snaps have been added to the *3D Object Snap* tab in the Drafting Settings dialog box and the 3D Object Snap options in the Status Bar.

- In a point cloud, you can use the **Object** option in the **UCS** command to align the active UCS to a plane.

- Dynamic UCS now aligns to a point cloud plane according to point density and alignment.

Attach Point Cloud

In the Attach Point Cloud dialog box, you can preview a point cloud and its detailed information (such as its classification and segmentation data) before attaching it, as shown in Figure 3–2. You can also use a geographic location for the attachment location (if the option is available).

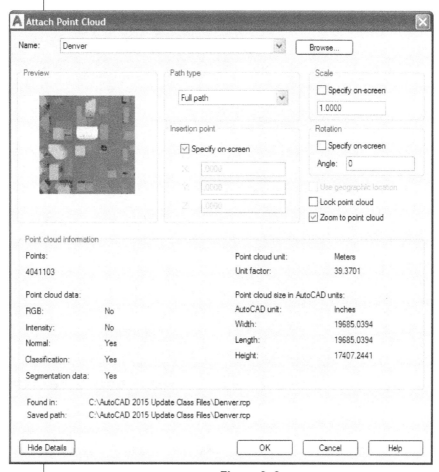

Figure 3–2

How To: Attach a Point Cloud

1. In the *Insert* tab>Point Cloud panel, click 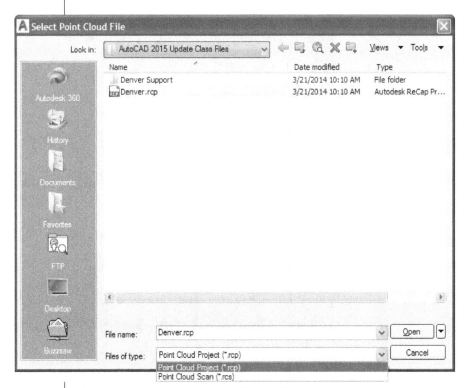 (Attach).
2. In the Select Point Cloud File dialog box, expand the Files of type drop-down list and select an option, as shown in Figure 3–3. In the *Name* area, select a file and click **Open**.

Figure 3–3

- The AutoCAD software can attach Point Cloud Project (RCP) and Scan (RCS) files (which are produced by the Autodesk ReCap software).

- The Autodesk ReCap software enables the creation of a point cloud project file (RCP) that references multiple indexed scan files (RCS). It converts scan file data into a point cloud format that can then be viewed and modified in other products.

3. In the Attach Point Cloud dialog box, click **Show Details** to display the point cloud information

4. In the *Path type*, *Insertion point*, *Scale*, and *Rotation* areas, set the options that you want to use to attach the point cloud, as shown in Figure 3–4. Click **OK**.

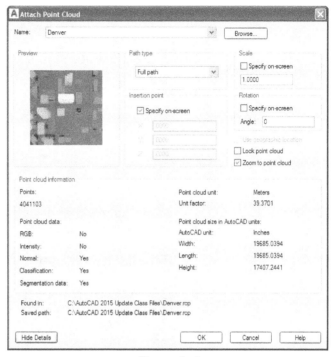

Figure 3–4

5. At the *Specify insertion point* prompt, click in the drawing to locate the point cloud.

Point Cloud Contextual Tab

When the point cloud has been attached, select it to display the *Point Cloud* contextual tab, as shown in Figure 3–5.

Figure 3–5

Display Panel

The Display panel enables you to control the size of the points in the point cloud using the Point Size slider, and the density of the points in all of the point clouds in the drawing using the Level of Detail slider, as shown in Figure 3–6. You can also access

 (Perspective), ⚓ (3D Orbit), 📷 (3D Swivel), and 👣 (3D Walk).

Figure 3–6

- The **AutoUpdate** command was removed as of the AutoCAD 2015 software.

Visualization Panel

In the Visualization panel, the options in the expanded Stylization drop-down list enable you to colorize the point cloud based on the **Scan Colors**, **Object Color**, **Normal** direction of a point, **Intensity** (reflectivity), **Elevation**, or **Classification**, as shown in Figure 3–7. The Point Cloud Color Map dialog box enables you to customize the colorization using the options in the *Intensity*, *Elevation*, and *Classification* tabs. You can also use the lighting tools to apply lighting effects to the point cloud.

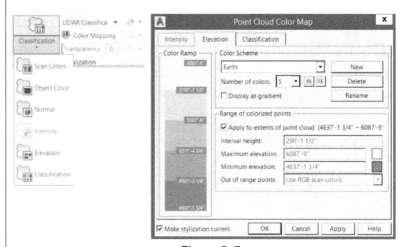

Figure 3–7

Point Cloud Transparency

When point clouds exist in a drawing with other geometry, it can be difficult to see anything behind the point cloud. A new tool in the *Point Cloud* contextual tab>Visualization panel enables you to adjusts the transparency of the point cloud, as shown in Figure 3–8. Alternatively, you can adjust the point cloud transparency in the Properties palette, as shown in Figure 3–8.

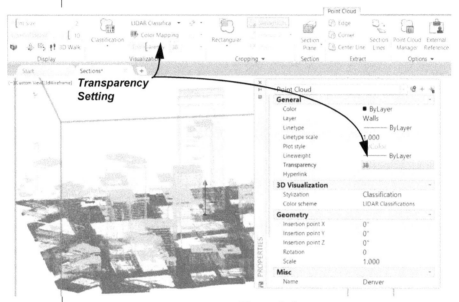

Figure 3–8

Cropping Panel

Displaying the bounding box around the point cloud data enables you to determine its position in 3D space relative to the other objects in the drawing. The cropping tools in the Cropping panel enable you to display only the information that is required for your project, as shown in Figure 3–9. The cropping boundary can be rectangular, circular, or polygonal and is normal to the screen. You can use ⊞ (Invert) to reverse the displayed points from inside to outside the boundary.

Figure 3–9

A new tool in the Cropping panel (displayed by expanding the panel) enables you to save and restore named cropping states. Both the visibility of the scans and regions as they are displayed and the cropping boundary are maintained in named cropping states, as shown in Figure 3–10.

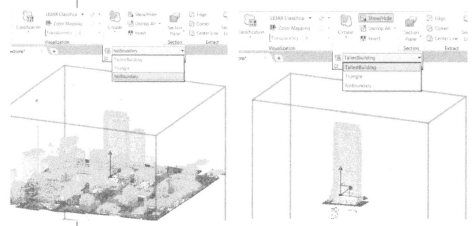

Figure 3–10

Hint: List Crop States

The new command **POINTCLOUDCROPSTATE** can be used to **S**ave, **R**estore, and **D**elete crop states, as shown in Figure 3–11. Using the **?** option will list all of the available crop states.

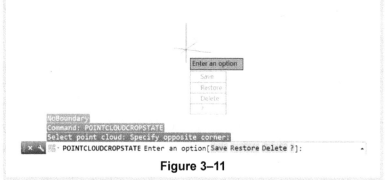

Figure 3–11

How To: Save a Named Crop State

1. Once a point cloud has been attached, select it in the model.
2. In the *Point Cloud* contextual tab>Cropping panel, select an appropriate crop boundary, as shown in Figure 3–12.

Figure 3–12

3. In the model, pick points to draw the boundary. If a Polygonal boundary was selected, press <Enter> when done.
4. At the cursor, select either **Inside** or **Outside** to indicate which points to keep.
5. Expand the *Point Cloud* contextual tab>Cropping panel, click

   (New Crop State).
6. Enter a name for the new crop state.

Section Panel

The new Section Plane drop-down tool can be found in the new Section panel of the contextual *Point Cloud* tab in the ribbon. It enables you to create section objects for the selected point cloud. Section objects can be created by specifying points or for different orthogonal orientations, as shown in Figure 3–13.

Figure 3–13

How To: Create a Point Cloud Section

1. Attach a point cloud, and select the point cloud in the model.
2. In the *Point Cloud* contextual tab>Section panel, click the down-arrow in the  (Section Plane).
3. Select the section orientation required.
4. Press <Esc> to release the point cloud selection.

Extract Panel

The new Extract panel (shown in Figure 3–14) enables you to create section lines from point clouds when live sectioning is toggled on.

Figure 3–14

When using the (Section Lines) command, linework can be extracted for the entire cross section or just for the perimeter. When creating section lines, settings can be adjusted to either speed up the creation process or make section line creation more accurate. The Extract Section Lines from Point Cloud dialog box is shown in Figure 3–15. The linework created from sections can be created on the active layer or a specific layer. Tolerances can be set to ensure lines meet a minimum length or have a specific connection and angle tolerance,

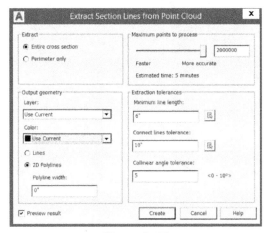

Figure 3–15

A process bar displays below the status bar, which indicates how much of the section generation process is complete, as shown in Figure 3–16.

Figure 3–16

Other tools in the Extract panel enable you to create one line at a time, as follows:

Icon	Command	Description
	Edge	Creates a line where two point cloud planer segments intersect.
	Corner	Extracts a point where three point cloud planer segments intersect.
	Centerline	Creates a line at the center of a cylindrical segment of a point cloud.

How To: Create Section Lines from Point Clouds

1. In the model, select the point cloud section line. In the contextual *Section Plane* tab>Display panel, verify that **Live Section** is toggled on, as shown in Figure 3–17.

Figure 3–17

2. Press <Esc> to release the section line.
3. In the model, select a point cloud that has a section already created.
4. In the *Point Cloud* contextual tab>Extract panel, click

    (Section Lines).

5. In the Extract Section Lines from Point Cloud dialog box, set the appropriate settings, as shown in Figure 3–18.

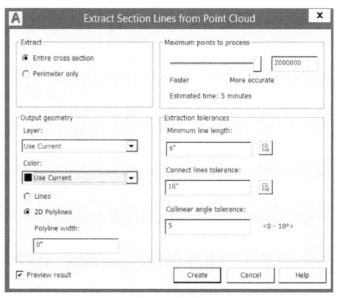

Figure 3–18

6. Click **Create**.

Options Panel

The Options panel (shown in Figure 3–19) enables you to access the Point Cloud Manager and External References Manager. You can use the Point Cloud Manager to modify multiple point clouds at the same time. A list of all of the point clouds in the drawing and their regions, unassigned points, and scans is displayed. You can toggle the objects on/off, rename, isolate, and highlight them in the drawing.

Figure 3–19

The Point Cloud Manager now includes on/off buttons for scans and regions, as shown in Figure 3–20 . Tooltips will always displays the full name of the scans and regions, since they can be truncated in order to display the new on/off button.

Figure 3–20

Object Snap

Point Cloud object snap modes have been added to the *3D Object Snap* tab of the Drafting Settings dialog box, as shown in Figure 3–21. They interpret faces and edges according to the point density and alignment.

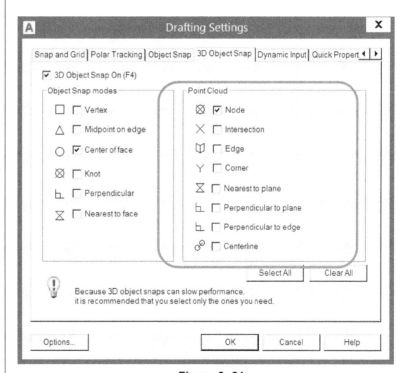

Figure 3–21

The point cloud object snaps are described as follows:

Icon	OSnap	Description
⊠	Node	Snaps to a point in a point cloud.
✕	Intersection	Snaps to the apparent intersection of 2 lines of a sectioned point cloud.
⬭	Edge	Snaps to the edge of two intersection planes.
Y	Corner	Snaps to the corner of 3 intersecting planes.
⊠	Nearest to plane	Snaps to any point in a plane.
⌐	Perpendicular to plane	Enables you to draw perpendicular to a plane.
⌐	Perpendicular to edge	Enables you to draw perpendicular to the edge of two intersecting planes.
⊘	Centerline	Snaps to the centerline of a cylindrical shape.

Dynamic UCS

Located in the Status Bar, ⊿ (Dynamic UCS) is a powerful tool that can help you draw using objects that are already in your model when drawing objects on temporary planes. Dynamic UCS now recognizes point cloud planes if the file includes segmentation data. The Properties palette indicates if the point cloud includes segmentation data, as shown in Figure 3–22.

Figure 3–22

How To: Use Dynamic UCS with Point Clouds

1. Verify that the point cloud file includes segmentation data in the Properties palette.

2. In the Status Bar, toggle on (Dynamic UCS).

3. In the Status Bar, toggle off all point cloud object snaps.

4. Start a draw command (circle, line, etc.)

5. Move the cursor over a point cloud face to highlight a plane and start drawing.

Practice 3a

Attach a Point Cloud

Practice Objectives

- Attach a point cloud when no other model exists for your project.
- Use the options in the Point Cloud contextual panel to modify the point cloud.

Estimated time for completion: 10 minutes

In this practice you will attach a point cloud to a new drawing file, as shown in Figure 3–23. You will then analyze it by changing the intensity color mapping.

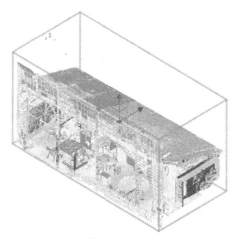

Figure 3–23

Task 1 - Attach a point cloud.

1. Start a new drawing.

2. In the *Insert* tab>Point Cloud panel, click (Attach).

3. In the Select Point Cloud File dialog box, navigate to your practice files folder.

4. Expand the Files of type drop-down list and note the available file formats. Select the **Point Cloud Scan (*.rcs)** file format.

5. In the *Name* area, select **787 Makerspace.rcs** and click **Open**.

6. Accept the default options in the Attach Point Cloud dialog box, click **OK**, and use an insertion point of **0,0**.

7. Save the file.

Task 2 - Analyze the point cloud.

Change the view to an isometric view for a better perspective.

1. Select the point cloud. The *Point Cloud* contextual tab displays.

2. In the ViewCube, select the **Top South West** corner to change the active view to an isometric view.

3. In the Visualization panel, expand the Stylization drop-down list and click ⌨ (Intensity).

4. The color scheme should display in multiple colors, as shown in Figure 3–24.

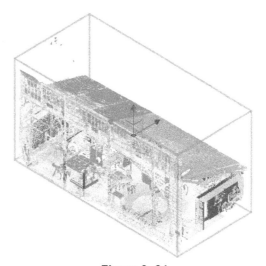

Figure 3–24

5. Save and close the file.

Practice 3b

Working with Sections

Practice Objective

* Create a section plane of a point cloud using the section commands.

Estimated time for completion: 10 minutes

In this practice you will create a section plane and then view the section of a point cloud. Next you will create section lines. The finished point cloud should look as shown in Figure 3–25.

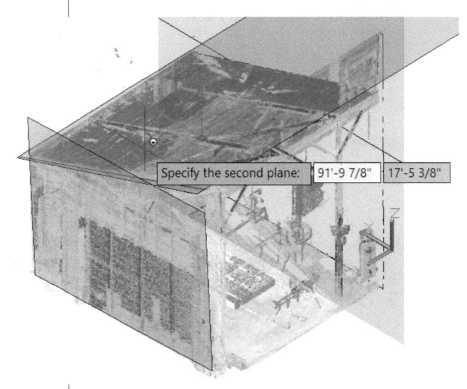

Specify the second plane: 91'-9 7/8"   17'-5 3/8"

Figure 3–25

1. Open **Sections.dwg** and switch to the **SW Isometric** view.

2. In the model, select the point cloud.

3. In the *Point Cloud* contextual tab>Section panel, click the down-arrow for ⬦ (Section Plane) and select ⬦ (Front).

4. The centroid of the point cloud is selected as a default, as shown in Figure 3–26.

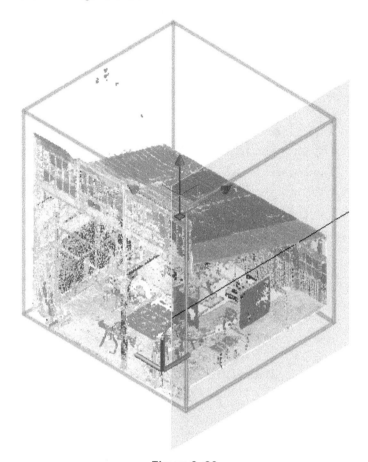

Figure 3–26

5. Press <Esc> to release the point cloud.

Verify that you type the foot symbol when typing in 22' as the drawing is in inches.

6. Select the new section plane. Right-click and verify that **Activate live sectioning** is checked. Use the Y-Gizmo to move the section plane **22'** to the North so that it cuts a section in the water heater, as shown in Figure 3–27. Press <Esc> to clear the selection and view the sectioned point cloud.

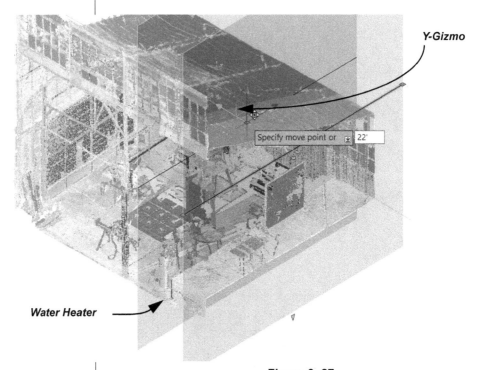

Figure 3–27

Task 3 - Extract linework from a point cloud.

1. In the *Home* tab>Layers panel, verify that the **Walls** layer is active.

2. In the model, select the point cloud.

3. In the *Point Cloud* contextual tab>Extract panel, click (Section Lines).

Note that it might take a few minutes to complete this process.

4. In the Extract Section Lines from Point Cloud dialog box, change the *Output geometry Color* to **ByLayer** and the *Maximum points to process* to about **50,000**, as shown in Figure 3–28. Leave all other settings to their default and click **Create**.

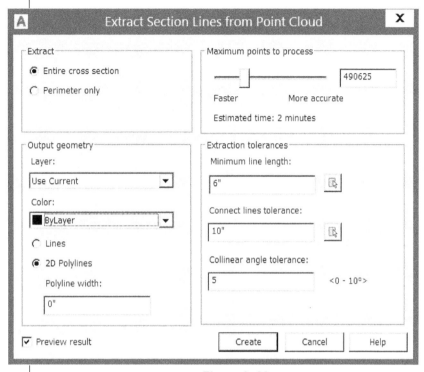

Figure 3–28

5. At the command line, select **Accept**.

6. With the Point Cloud still selected, in the *Point Cloud* contextual tab>Visualization panel, change the Transparency to about **50%** to make it easier to see the new linework.

7. Change the view to the **NW Isometric** view.

8. Select the point cloud again, if it is no longer selected.

9. In the *Point Cloud* contextual tab>Extract panel, click (Edge).

10. In the model, click the north wall and the roof for the planes to create an edge from, as shown in Figure 3–29.

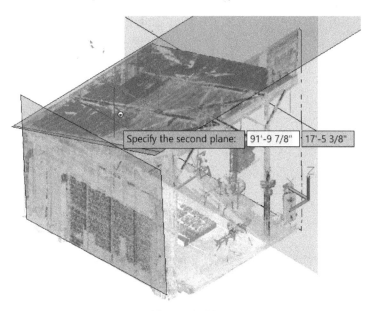

Specify the second plane: | 91'-9 7/8" | 17'-5 3/8"

Figure 3–29

11. If time permits, try drawing linework using the point cloud object snap options.

12. Save and close the drawing.

3.2 Rendering

Rendering has been simplified with a new render engine. The new physically based path tracing renderer produces better results.

While you can display important 3D information using visual styles, materials, lights, and shadows, you sometimes need to create a more refined view to present to clients. You can do this by creating a rendered image, as shown in How To:Figure 3–30. Creating rendered images takes time and skill, but you can do a few things to quickly obtain a rendering.

- Rendering tools are located in the 3D Modeling workspace in the *Visualize* tab>Render panel.

Figure 3–30

When selecting a render preset, hover the cursor over the preset to see how long the view is rendered for or how many rendering levels are applied, as shown in Figure 3–31.

Figure 3–31

How To: Render a View

1. Set up the view with lights, materials, and shadows.
2. In the Render Presets Control, select an option as shown in Figure 3–32.

Figure 3–32

3. In *the Visualize* tab>Render panel, click (Render). The entire scene is rendered based on the Render Presets. By default, the Render window opens displaying the results.

• In the *Visualize* tab>Render panel, expand **Render in** and select **Render in Region** to only render a selected area in the drawing window. Click (Render to Size) and pick a crop window to render. Use this when you are testing materials and lights. Type **Regen** or select a named or preset view to return to the drawing window.

• Select **Render in Window**) in the *Visualize* tab> Render panel. Then click (Render to Size) to open the Render window in which you can preview, print, and save renderings.

• Expand (Render to Size) to select the render output size and quality, as shown in Figure 3–33.

Figure 3–33

4. Click (Render to Size) to open the Render Window and start the rendering process.

How To: Save a Rendering to a File

1. In the *Visualize* tab>Render panel, click (Render to Size) to open the Render window.

   Alternatively, in the *Visualize* tab>expanded Render panel,

   click (Render Window).

2. In the Render window, click (Save).
3. In the Render Output File dialog box, assign a name, location, and file format. File formats include BMP, TGA, TIF, JPEG, and PNG. Click **Save**.
4. In the Image Options dialog box, select the color quality and click **OK**. For example, the dialog box for PNG is shown in Figure 3–34.

Figure 3–34

Adjusting the Exposure

Click  (Render Environment and Exposure) in the *Visualize* tab>expanded Render panel to modify the brightness and contrast of the active view. You can also change the White Balance and background options, as shown in Figure 3–35. The active view displays the changes.

Figure 3–35

Render Presets Manager

Additional presets can be added or modified using  (Render Presets Manager) in the *View* tab>Palettes panel. The Render Presets Manager palette opens in which you can set options, such as render size, render duration, and render accuracy, as shown in Figure 3–36. If you know that you are going to render a view many times using similar settings, you should create a new Render Preset.

Figure 3–36

How To: Create Render Presets

1. In the *Visualize* tab>Render panel, click 📐 (Render Presets Manager).
2. In the Render Presets Manager palette, select an existing preset that is similar to the one you want to create and click

   ⚙ (Create Copy).
3. If required, modify the settings, as shown in Figure 3–37.

Figure 3–37

4. Close the Render Presets Manager. In the Render Presets Control, set the new preset to be active before rendering.

Practice 3c

Rendering Concepts

Estimated time for completion: 5 minutes

Practice Objective

- Render a view using the Draft preset and then render a region of a view using a higher preset.

In this practice you will render a view using the **Low** preset and then render a view again using a higher preset, such as the one shown in Figure 3–38. If time permits, you can render a region using a higher setting.

Figure 3–38

1. Open **Condo-With-Skylight-M.dwg**.

2. Change the workspace to **3D Modeling**.

3. In the *Home* tab>View panel, switch to the **Render View_330pm** view.

4. In the *Visualize* tab>expanded Render panel, click
   ♦ (Render Environment and Exposure).

5. In the Render Environment & Exposure palette, set the following:
   - *Environment*: **On**
   - *Image Based Lighting*: **Sharp Highlights**
   - *Exposure*: **15** (Dark)
   - *White Balance*: **7829** (Cool)
   - Leave all other defaults, as shown in Figure 3–39.

Figure 3–39

6. Close the Render Environment & Exposure palette.

7. In the *Visualize* tab>Render panel, set the *Render Preset* to **Low**, expand (Render to Size) and select **800 x 600 px - SVGA**.

8. In the *Visualize* tab>Render panel, click (Render to Size). The Render dialog box opens and the view is rendered quickly, but not very effectively, as shown in Figure 3–40.

Figure 3–40

9. Change the *Render Preset* to **High**.

10. In the *Visualize* tab>Render panel, click  (Render to Size). The Render dialog box opens and the view is rendered, as shown in Figure 3–41. The process takes longer but you can see the materials, lights, and shadows much more clearly.

Figure 3–41

11. Save and close the drawing.

Chapter Review Questions

1. You cannot insert Point Cloud Project (RCP) or Scan (RCS) files into the AutoCAD software.

   a. True

   b. False

2. Where are the Point Cloud Object Snap modes found?

   a. *Snap and Grid* tab of the Drafting Settings dialog box

   b. *Object Snap* tab of the Drafting Settings dialog box

   c. *3D Object Snap* tab of the Drafting Settings dialog box

   d. Contextual *Point Cloud* tab>Object Snap panel

3. How can you automatically create linework from point clouds?

   a. Use any of the commands in the contextual *Point Cloud* tab>Extract panel.

   b. When inserting the point cloud, select the option to create linework.

   c. In the Point Cloud Manager, right-click on the scan name and select **Create Linework**.

   d. You cannot create linework automatically for point clouds.

4. How do you estimate how long the view will take to render or how many times rendering levels will be applied?

   a. There is no way to estimate that.

   b. In the Render window, right-click and select **Render Time**.

   c. In the *Visualize* tab>expanded Render panel, click **Render Environment and Exposure**.

   d. When selecting a render preset, hover the cursor over the preset.

5. What are the six default Render Presets?

    a. Draft Quality, Medium Quality, Presentation Quality, Coffee Break Quality, Lunch Quality, and Overnight Quality

    b. Low, Medium, High, Coffee Break Quality, Lunch Quality, and Overnight Quality.

    c. Low, Medium, High, Draft, Presentation, Video

    d. There are only three default Render Presets: Draft Quality, Medium Quality, Presentation Quality

Command Summary

Button	Command	Location
	Attach Point Cloud	• **Ribbon:** *Insert* tab>Point Cloud panel • **Command Prompt:** pointcloudattach
	Autodesk Recap	• **Ribbon:** *Insert* tab>Point Cloud panel • **Command Prompt:** recap
	Dynamic UCS	• Status Bar
	Extract Centerline	• **Ribbon:** *Point Cloud* contextual tab>Extract panel • Command Prompt: pcextractcenterline
	Extract Corner	• **Ribbon:** *Point Cloud* contextual tab>Extract panel • **Command Prompt:** pcextractcorner
	Extract Edge	• **Ribbon:** *Point Cloud* contextual tab>Extract panel • **Command Prompt:** pcextractedge
	Extract Section	• **Ribbon:** *Point Cloud* contextual tab>Extract panel • **Command Prompt:** pcextractsection
	Render	• **Ribbon:** *Visualize* tab>Render panel • **Command Prompt:** render
	Render Window	• **Ribbon:** *Visualize* tab>Render panel • **Command Prompt:** renderwindow
	Render Environment and Exposure	• **Ribbon:** *Visualize* tab>Render panel • **Command Prompt:** renderexposure
	Save Render	• **Window:** Render

Chapter

4

Building Information Modeling and Cloud Tools

In this chapter you learn how teams can work together and share information. You explore Autodesk® 360, the direct connection to the Autodesk 360 environment in which drawings can be stored for others to easily access. You also learn how to use building information modeling to coordinate models and collaborate with others on the project design team.

Learning Objectives in this Chapter

- Connect to the Autodesk 360 environment and social networking sites to improve productivity.
- Attach Autodesk® Navisworks® files.
- Attach models from Autodesk® BIM 360™ Glue®.

4.1 Connecting to the Cloud

The AutoCAD software Help makes collaboration easier and more effective. A360 enables you to use a Cloud environment to connect and share files directly from the AutoCAD software. You can also connect directly to Autodesk social communities from the software.

Stay Connected Menu

In the InfoCenter, you can use the Stay Connected drop-down list to access the Autodesk Subscription Center, Autodesk Certified Hardware, and various social networking sites, as shown in Figure 4–1. In the *AutoCAD on the web* area, select **AutoCAD Blog, YouTube, Facebook,** or **Twitter**, to follow the latest news and get the latest tips and tricks for the Autodesk software.

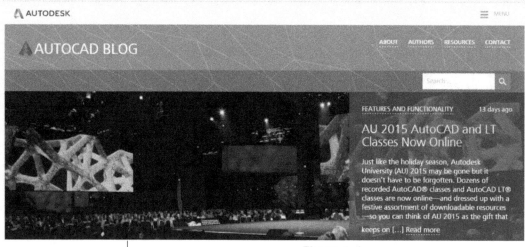

Figure 4–1

A360 Login and Settings

When you log into A360 for the first time, you might need to create an account. Doing so is free and provides you with 25 GB of free space for storing drawings and settings. Expand the Sign In drop-down list in the InfoCenter (as shown in Figure 4–2) and select **Sign In to Autodesk account**. You are prompted to sign in using your Autodesk ID, or you can create an ID by clicking **Signing up**.

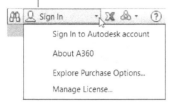 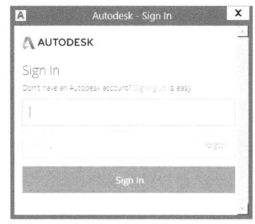

Figure 4–2

- Once you have logged in, your sign in name displays in the *A360* area, in the InfoCenter.

Expand the Sign In name drop-down list to display the options for working in the cloud, as shown in Figure 4–3. The **Sync my settings with the cloud** option enables you to save local settings to the cloud and be able to use them if you log in from different locations.

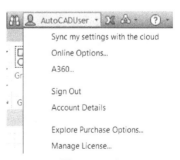

Figure 4–3

The *A360* tab (shown in Figure 4–4) includes many of the online tools that are used for cloud collaboration.

Figure 4–4

Click ⌐ in the *A360* tab>Settings Sync panel to open the Options dialog box in the *Online* tab, as shown in Figure 4–5. You can enable the automatic sync and determine which settings are synced with the cloud. If you select the **Sync my settings with the cloud** option, a copy of every drawing you save is saved in your *A360* folder.

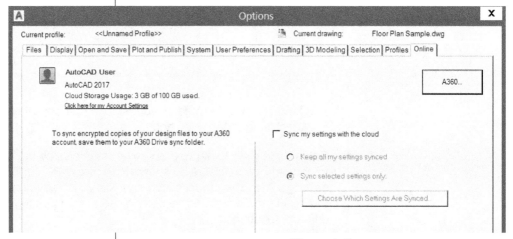

Figure 4–5

Click ⌐ (Choose Settings) in the *A360* tab>Settings Sync panel to log in to A360 on different computers and use the same interface appearance, profiles, workspaces, options, and support files. The options that can be synced are shown in Figure 4–6. A bubble notification prompts you when the settings are being uploaded/downloaded from the cloud.

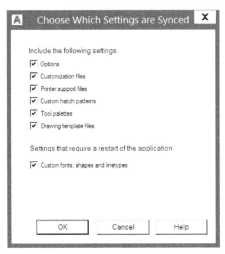

Figure 4–6

Design Feed

The Design Feed palette has been removed from the ribbon. However, it can still be accessed by typing DESIGNFEEDOPEN. It enables you to share text messages and attached images online with others using A360 or your company's network, as shown in Figure 4–7. You can access Design Feed messages from the internet, a mobile device, or your computer. You can store drawing files associated with Design Feed in A360, on your computer, or on your company's network.

Figure 4–7

- Design Feed enables you to associate a message with a specific area in a drawing. That area is then identified with

  . If you select a message in the Design Feed, it zooms to the related area in the drawing. You can control how the bubbles display using the options in the Settings drop-down list in the Design Feed palette.

- If you tag other users in your message they receive a notification by email and in Design Feed.

- All posts are saved with the associated drawing and any images, to your A360 account, where authorized people can view it, and post replies.

- When message threads are finished, you can hide them by clicking ✔ (Resolve).

- If you save an associated drawing with another name, you can also save its Design Feed comments. In the Save Drawing As dialog box, select the **Copy Design Feed from previous version** option.

- If you are using eTransmit, DWG Convert, or Archive to copy an associated drawing, you can select the **Remove Design Feed** option to remove any Design Feed information from the drawing.

Sharing Drawings in the Cloud

Sharing drawings with other team members in A360 is as easy as saving the drawing file and selecting **A360** as the storage location in the Save in drop-down list, as shown in Figure 4–8.

Additionally, you can click ⬚ (Share Document) on the *A360* tab>Share panel. You can also open files from the Cloud and attach files located in the Cloud using the Look in drop-down list and selecting the **A360** option.

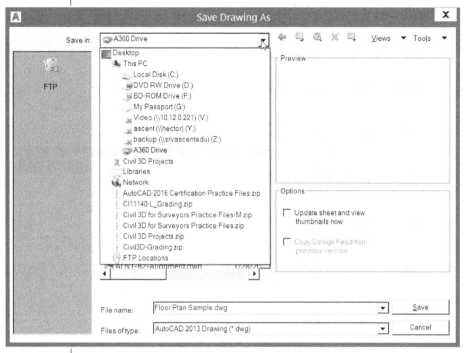

Figure 4–8

Upload Drawings

After signing into A360, click ![icon](Open A360 Drive) in the *A360* tab>Online Files panel to open the A360 browser, which displays a list of the folders available.

- Navigate into the folders to locate files as required.

- Click **Upload** in the A360 browser to upload one or more files at a time.

Sharing Files

Public sharing enables anyone to access a drawing that has the link. The link enables them to display or download the drawing without permitting them to make changes. Private sharing enables you to share drawings with other users with whom you are actively working on projects. This enables them to display, download, and edit any drawings to which you provide access. The link is created in the Share dialog box, as shown in Figure 4–9.

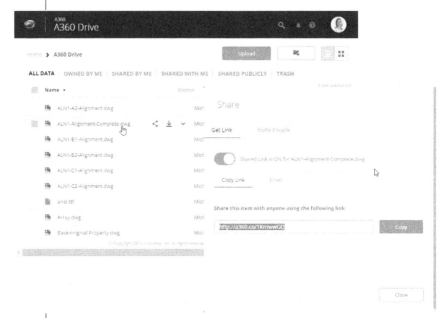

Figure 4–9

To correctly display drawings in A360, you must use a browser that supports HTML 5.

• When you hover over a drawing name, icons display that enable you to work with the file, as shown in Figure 4–9. These icons are described in the table below.

• Click on a drawing to preview it in a web browser.

❮	**Share:** Enables you to share a link with other users so that they can access the file in A360.
↓	**Download:** Enables you to download the file for local viewing and editing.

Enables you to move, copy, rename, upload a new version, or delete the file.

Share Design View

To publish views of drawings to the cloud while protecting your drawing files, on the *A360* tab>Share panel, click  (Share Design View). Using this option enables stakeholders to view the design without having to log into A360 or have the AutoCAD software on their computer. The **Design View** command is also located in the Application Menu, as shown in Figure 4–10.

Figure 4–10

4.2 Rendering in the Cloud

The A360 panel in the *Visualize* tab in the 3D Modeling workspace provides options for rendering drawings in the cloud while you continue to work on other drawings. Click ⬡ (Render in Cloud) to render up to four drawing views at a time using Cloud space to process your work. In the Autodesk 360 dialog box you can select the model views that you want to render in the cloud, as shown in Figure 4–11. You are prompted when the renderings are complete and can also be notified by email.

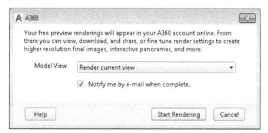

Figure 4–11

- In the *Visualize* tab>A360 panel, click 🖼 (Render Gallery) to browse your online render gallery.

Practice 4a

Working in A360

Practice Objectives

- Render a drawing without using your computer's processor by using the Render in the Cloud command.
- Upload drawings and other files to A360 to easily share them with others.

Estimated time for completion: 10 minutes

In this practice you will upload drawings to A360 and render a view in the cloud while continuing to work on your computer.

Task 1 - Render in the cloud.

1. In the InfoCenter, select **Sign In to A360** and type your Autodesk ID and password.

   - If you do not have an Autodesk ID, select **Signing up** and create an account as shown in Figure 4–12.

Figure 4–12

2. Open **Kitchen-Materials.dwg** from your practice files folder.

3. Verify that you are in the 3D Modeling workspace.

4. In the *Visualize* tab>Views panel, select the **Dining Area** view.

5. In the *Visualize* tab>Render panel, set the *Render Preset* to **High**.

6. Save the drawing.

7. In the *Visualize* tab>A360 panel, click  (Render in Cloud).

If the Render Online -
Save Changes warning
box opens, click OK to
save the drawing.

8. In the A360 dialog box, expand the Model View drop-down list and select **Render current view**. Clear the **Notify me by e-mail when complete** option and click **Start Rendering**.

9. The rendering is created in the background as you continue working. You can check the status of the rendering by expanding your A360 name in the InfoCenter. If the drawing is still being rendered it displays **Rendering in Progress** at the bottom of the drop-down list, as shown in Figure 4–13. It also displays a rotating circle next to your A360 name.

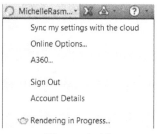

Figure 4–13

Task 2 - Upload files to A360.

1. In the *A360* tab>Online Files panel, Click (Open A360 Drive) to open the A360 browser.

2. In the browser, click **Upload**.

3. Navigate to your practice files folder and select only the drawing files in the directory to upload. Hold <Shift> or <Ctrl> to select multiple files. Click **Open** to complete the upload process.

4. In the AutoCAD software, start a new drawing.

5. Click (Application Menu) and select **Save As**.

6. In the Save in drop-down list, select **A360 Drive**. Name the drawing **Cloud.dwg** and then click **Save**.

7. Close the drawing.

8. In the A360 browser, select all of the drawings by putting a check at the top of the select column.

9. Click (Delete) to remove the drawings from the cloud.

10. Close the A360 browser.

4.3 Attaching Navisworks Files

Navisworks software enables architecture, engineering, and construction professionals to integrate models from multiple software origins. Integrating models into one model ensures better communication to resolve conflicts, coordinate disciplines, and plan projects before construction begins. The AutoCAD software now has the capability to attach Navisworks (NWD or NWC) files for project coordination purposes. The **2D Endpoint** and **Center** object snap commands now work on coordination models. The same tools used to attach external reference files are used to attach Navisworks files.

> **Hint: Supported Systems**
>
> Navisworks files can only be attached using 64-bit systems with hardware acceleration toggled on.

How To: Attach Navisworks Files

1. Open the External Reference palette. Expand the Attach drop-down list and select **Attach Coordination Model**, as shown in Figure 4–14.

    Alternatively, in the *Insert* tab>Reference panel, click

     (Attach).

Figure 4–14

2. In the Select Reference File dialog box, select **Navisworks files** from the Files of type drop-down list, as shown in Figure 4–15.

Figure 4–15

3. Select the required file and click **Open**.
4. In the Attach Coordination Model dialog box (shown in Figure 4–16), set the following:
   - Path type
   - Insertion point
   - Scale
   - Rotation
   - Display options

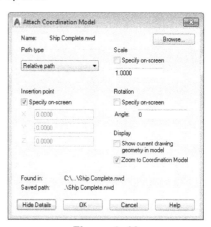

Figure 4–16

5. Click **OK** to attach the file and complete the command.

Hint: Avoid Geometry Duplication

If the active drawing is part of the Navisworks model, you can hide that part of the model during the attach process. Simply uncheck the option **Show current drawing geometry in model** in the Attach Coordination Model dialog box.

Coordination Model Contextual Tab

The *Coordination Model* contextual tab provides a number of tools to help you navigate and correctly display any attached Navisworks models, as shown in Figure 4–17. The tools are described as follows.

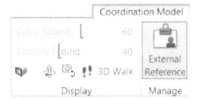

Figure 4–17

Button	Command	Description
	3D Orbit	Orbits the view around a 3D model.
	3D Swivel	Simulates the effect of turning a camera to change the view.
	3D Walk	Changes the 3D view interactively to create the appearance of walking through the model.
		Use the following keys to help you navigate:
		• W (forward)
		• A (left)
		• S (back)
		• D (right)
		OR
		Use the mouse to specify the view direction.
	Color Fading	Controls the amount of black blended geometry and attached coordination models.
	Opacity Fading	Controls the amount of dimming through transparency.
	Perspective	Changes the active view from an orthogonal view to a perspective view.

Practice 4b

Estimated time for completion: 10 minutes

Attach a Navisworks File

Practice Objective

- Attach an Autodesk Navisworks file.

In this practice you will attach and view an Autodesk Navisworks model to an AutoCAD drawing file.

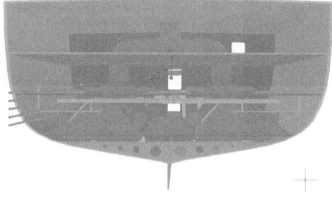

Figure 4–18

Task 1 - Attach a Navisworks file.

1. Start a new drawing file from the default AutoCAD template.

2. In the *Insert* tab>Reference panel, click 🗔 (Attach).

3. In the Select Reference File dialog box, select **Navisworks files** from the Files of type drop-down list, as shown in Figure 4–19.

Figure 4–19

4. Select **Ship Complete.nwd** from the practice files directory and click **Open**.

5. In the Attach Coordination Model dialog box accept all of the defaults, as shown in Figure 4–20.

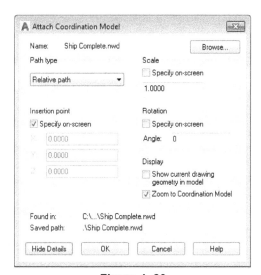

Figure 4–20

6. Click **OK** to attach the file

7. For the insertion point, type **0,0,0** and click <Enter> to complete the command.

Task 2 - View the coordination model.

1. In the model, select the attached coordination model.

2. In the *Coordination Model* contextual tab>Display panel, click
    ⚓ (3D Orbit).

3. In the model, click and drag a point with the cursor to view the
    model from other angles. Press <Esc> when done.

4. In the ViewCube, click **Back** to view the back side of the
    coordination model.

5. In the *Coordination Model* contextual tab>Display panel, click
    ◧ (Perspective).

6. In the *Coordination Model* contextual tab>Display panel, click
    ‼ (3D Walk). Using the keyboard:

    *   Press <W> to move forward.
    *   Press <A> to move left.
    *   Press <S> to move back.
    *   Press <D> to move right.

7. Press <Esc> when done.

8. Close the file without saving.

4.4 Attaching BIM 360 Glue Models

Autodesk® BIM 360™ Glue® is a cloud-based BIM management and collaboration product for construction collaboration. Autodesk BIM 360 Glue models (single or merged) can now be attached to AutoCAD drawings to assist in project collaboration.

How To: Attach BIM 360 Models

Since BIM 360 Models are cloud and subscription based, you must be logged into an A360 account that has access to BIM 360 Glue, in order to see the BIM 360 tab.

1. Login to your A360 account in the Communication Center.

2. In the *BIM 360* tab>Coordination panel, click ⊹ (Attach).

3. In the Append dialog box, select the BIM 360 Glue model to attach, as shown in Figure 4–21.

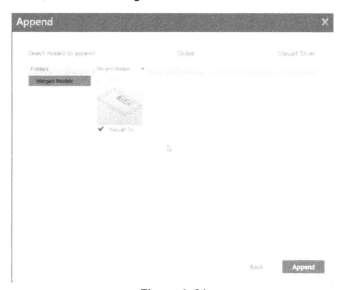

Figure 4–21

4. Click **Append**.

5. Enter the required value for each of the following, pressing <Enter> between each entry.
   - insertion point
   - scale
   - rotation angle.

> **Hint: Automatic Loading**
>
> When the drawing is re-opened, the latest version of the BIM 360 Glue model is automatically loaded.

Chapter Review Questions

1. How much storage space is provided by default in A360 when you create an account?

   a. 1 MB

   b. 10 GB

   c. 25 GB

   d. 250 GB

2. What does the **Stay Connected** menu enable you to access?

   a. Your A360 account.

   b. AutoCAD WS.

   c. Autodesk Recap.

   d. Product updates, Autodesk Subscription Center, Facebook, and Twitter.

3. What happens when you save settings in the cloud?

   a. Causes your settings, AutoCAD Profile, and other configuration files to sync across all computers.

   b. They save in your Autodesk software as well.

   c. You can share them with others.

   d. You need to reset them after each sign-in.

4. You cannot save a file directly to the Cloud.

   a. True

   b. False

5. In A360, how do you upload a drawing to the Cloud?

   a. Click **Save**.

   b. Click **Share**.

   c. Click **Upload**.

   d. You must do it in the AutoCAD software.

6. What are the new types of files that can now be attached in the External References palette?

   a. MicroStation files

   b. PDF files

   c. Navisworks files

   d. Drawing files

7. Attaching a coordination model is supported on 32-bit systems.

   a. True

   b. False

8. If the BIM 360 ribbon tab is hidden, it could be due to the following reasons. (Select all that apply)

   a. You are not logged into an A360 account.

   b. Your A360 account does not have access to BIM 360 Glue.

   c. The ribbon tab might be toggled off.

   d. None of the above.

Command Summary

Button	Command	Location
	3D Orbit	• **Ribbon:** *Coordination Model* contextual tab>Display panel
	3D Swivel	• **Ribbon:** *Coordination Model* contextual tab>Display panel
	3D Walk	• **Ribbon:** *Coordination Model* contextual tab>Display panel
	Attach	• **Ribbon:** *Insert* tab>Reference panel • **Palette:** External References
	Attach BIM 360 Glue Model	• **Ribbon:** BIM 360 tab>Coordination panel
N/A	**Color Fading**	• **Ribbon:** *Coordination Model* contextual tab>Display panel
	Open A360 Drive	• **Ribbon:** *A360* tab>Online Files panel
N/A	**Opacity Fading**	• **Ribbon:** *Coordination Model* contextual tab>Display panel
	Perspective	• **Ribbon:** *Coordination Model* contextual tab>Display panel
	Share Design View	• **Ribbon:** *A360* tab>Share panel
	Share Document	• **Ribbon:** *A360* tab>Share panel

Index

---

www.ingramcontent.com/pod-product-compliance
Lightning Source LLC
LaVergne TN
LVHW062317060326
832902LV00013B/2275